The Random House Book of

Old Roses

By

ROGER PHILLIPS
& MARTYN RIX

Design Jill Bryan, Gill Stokoe & Debby Curry

RANDOM HOUSE

Acknowledgements

Most of the roses photographed came from the following gardens and we are grateful to the staff of these gardens for their help:
The National Trust, Mottisfont; The Gardens of the Rose, St Albans; Hidcote Manor, Gloustershire; Longleat House, Wiltshire; Roseraie de L'Haÿ-les-Roses; David Austin Roses; Jardin exotique du Val Rahmeh, Menton; Eccleston Square Gardens, The Sangerhausen Rosarium, Germany.

Among others who have helped in one way or another we would like to thank: William Waterfield, Fred Boutin, Graham Thomas, Odile Mesqualier, Miriam Rothschild, Mrs Barlow, Marilyn Inglis, Amanda Bryan and Anne Thatcher.

Published in the United States by Random House, Inc., New York.
This work was originally published in Great Britain by Pan, an imprint of Macmillan Publishers Limited, in 1998 as *The Pan Plant Chooser Series Traditional Old Roses*.
ISBN 0-375-75196-3

Random House website address:
www.randomhouse.com

Printed in Great Britain
9 8 7 6 5 4 3 2
First U.S. Edition

Colour Reproduction by Aylesbury Studios Ltd.
Printed by Butler and Tanner Ltd. Frome, Somerset

Contents

Roses in an old courtyard in Bokhara

What is an Old Rose

What is an Old Rose, or an Old Garden Rose as they are often called? That is a difficult question and it is much easier to say what it is not. It is not a rose bred for exhibition at a rose show or for the florists' shop. It is not a rose designed for bedding, to fill a bed with the brightest and most reliable colour over the longest season. It is not a rose designed to produce the glossiest, healthiest leaves, or the largest, most perfect flower. Generally, too, it is not a recent rose raised in the last fifty years; in fact most of the roses in this book were raised over a hundred years ago. They are genuine antiques; '*Roses Anciennes*', as they are called in France, or 'Heritage Roses', as they are often called in America.

Old Roses are survivors. They have survived because they are tough and not easy to kill, because they are loved and handed around among friends or down the generations. Most are easy to grow and root from cuttings, and although they may get disease, their flowering is undiminished.

Some of the roses shown here are of recent breeding, but are included because they conform to the style of the old varieties and associate well with them in the garden. One important group of these modern 'Old Roses' has been largely omitted, as they could well be the subject of a separate book of this size. These are David Austin's 'English Roses', which set out to re-create the shapes, soft colours and good scent of the Old Roses, combined with continuous flowering and disease-resistance of modern roses *(page 20)*. Several of these English Roses have almost achieved classic status already, and David Austin's work has been so successful that other breeders are copying him.

'Heritage', one of David Austin's roses with similarities to a Bourbon.

INTRODUCTION

Rosa phoenicia, a possible parent of the Damask roses, growing over an olive tree in south Turkey

The roses in this book are grouped according to their supposed relationships. 'Supposed' because many are ancient garden plants from China, Persia or Turkey, and their likely descent from wild species roses has been deduced from the details of their structure, their chromosomes and from the possible ancestors available in the area where they are thought to have originated.

Modern DNA analysis may be able to unravel some of the outstanding questions about Old Rose parentage, but that is complicated and expensive work which still needs to be done. It may then be possible to prove the true parentage of the Damask roses, whether they are derived from the ancient cultivated Musk rose or the wild Turkish *Rosa phoenicia*.

Rosa gallica wild in the south of France, with single deep pink and intensely scented flowers

Rosa phoenicia

The house at Malmaison today; here Joséphine began her collection of roses

Old Roses in History

Roses have been appreciated, collected and grown in gardens, above all other flowers, for thousands of years. Many individuals in history, though bloodthirsty and ruthless, are remembered as lovers of roses. Sultan Mehmet the Conqueror (of Constantinople in 1453) is shown in a famous miniature at the Topkapi Museum in Istanbul, sniffing a red *gallica*, probably 'Officinalis'; this was often known as the Red Damask Rose. The roses of medieval gardens came to Europe from the East, brought both by returning crusaders and by visitors to the Ottoman court.

The Empress Joséphine, wife of Napoléon, collected all the roses she could and grew them in the garden at Malmaison. She comissioned P. J. Redouté to paint them, and her collection and his paintings, published as *Les Roses*, 1817–24, have become the starting point for our scientific knowledge of garden roses, as well as the source of numerous illustrations for waste paper baskets, table mats, etc. Josephine's patronage led to a great enthusiasm for roses in France, and French breeders were pre-eminent throughout the 19th century. Most of the roses in this book were raised in France. Since then, rose breeding has become more widespread, and large breeders are now based in England, North America, Germany and New Zealand as well France.

The 20th Century

The appreciation and collecting of Old Roses, or Antique roses in contrast to rose breeding, has gathered pace during the 20th century. In 1902, in *Roses for English Gardens*, Gertrude Jekyll extolled the virtues of the old cottage shrubs, the Centifolias and Gallicas. In the early 1920s, while the main rose breeders were concentrating on producing exhibition roses, the Rev. Joseph Pemberton was raising his now famous Hybrid Musks (*shown on pages 80-83*). In *Old Garden Roses*, published in 1936, Edward Bunyard traced the history of roses through the ages and described those that were still grown in England.

Graham Thomas, through his writings and his work with the National Trust is the leading light of the recent craze for Old Roses. He brought together collections made

INTRODUCTION

Roses trained on larch poles at the Sangerhausen Rosarium, Germany

by famous gardeners such as Vita Sackville-West at Sissinghurst and the Countess of Rosse at Nymans, grew and distributed them while at Hillings Nursery and finally donated his collection to Mottisfont Garden, where it can be studied today. Graham Thomas's work in collecting Old Roses has been continued by Peter Beales who sells most of them through his nursery in Attleborough, Norfolk.

In America, the Texas Rose Rustlers and other Heritage rose groups, have saved many Old Roses from extinction, by gathering them from old country cemeteries and abandoned gardens. One of the largest collections of these was set up by Fred Boutin, the authority on the Old Roses of California, in the Huntington Gardens at San Merino, near Los Angeles; here it can be studied and any found roses can be compared with the named varieties in the garden.

The largest and one of the most remarkable collections of roses in Europe is at Sangerhausen in northeast Germany. Here a collection built up in the early 20th century, has been faithfully preserved though war and political adversity. Many Old Roses have been preserved only here, and a visit to the garden is a notable experience.

A hedge of Hybrid Musk roses

Alba Roses

The Alba roses form large shrubs with bluish grey leaves and usually white or pale pink, wonderfully scented flowers. They are of doubtful origin, but certainly very ancient, probably grown by the Romans and certainly well known by medieval times when they were associated with the Virgin Mary. They flower only in midsummer, but have a long season and when well grown, the whole bush is covered with flowers.

All the Alba roses are very hardy, as would be expected of plants which are probably crosses between wild Dog roses and ancient Damasks. They do not suffer from blackspot, and some can get rust which disfigures the leaves after flowering, but otherwise does not seem to affect next year's flowering. Although Alba roses will thrive in poor soil, they do best when well fed, especially when first planted.

PLANTING & PRUNING HELP   All roses are best planted from bare root plants in winter. Do not be afraid to cut back the roots of roses to 8in (20cm) or even down to 6in (15cm). They sprout vigorously from the cut ends, therefore it is best to keep the roots short and straight, not coiled around in the planting hole. The garden value of these robust, once-flowering roses can be extended by planting a delicate clematis, such as *Clematis viticella* 'Alba Luxurians', which climbs

A large bush of *Rosa × alba* 'Semiplena'

'Great Maiden's Blush'

ALBA ROSES

Rosa × alba 'Semiplena'

over it and begins to flower after the roses have finished. Albas do not need pruning every year, but can be tidied and reduced in size every five years by cutting out old poorly growing branches. Hardy to −30°F (−35°C), US zones 4–8.

'Jacobite Rose', *Rosa × alba* 'Maxima', 'Great Double White'   A large shrub with arching branches to 7ft (2m) long. The pure white flowers have a hint of pink in the centre at first, with a mass of irregular curled inner petals, showing a few stamens. This has been known to revert to 'Semiplena' (*described below*). Good scent.

***Rosa × alba* 'Semiplena'**   A large shrub with arching branches to 8ft (2.5m). The pure white flowers are about 3in (8cm) across with loose outer petals, showing a boss of yellow stamens. The scent is very good, and in some places this rose is grown in place of the usual Damask rose to produce Attar of Roses. It will thrive anywhere except in deep shade.

'Great Maiden's Blush', 'Cuisse de Nymphe', 'La Séduisante'   A large shrub to 8ft (2.5m) tall, and more across, suckering when grown on its own roots. Leaflets dark bluish green, paler

beneath. Flowers about 3in (8cm) across, very double, palest pink outside, flushed deeper in the middle, with a tiny green eye, showing only a few stamens when fully open, finally fading to white. This is another ancient variety, known at least since the 15th century, with a wonderful scent, less heavy than that of the Damasks.

'Jacobite Rose'

'Mme Legras de St Germain'

'Félicité Parmentier'

'Céleste', 'Celestial' A very delicate and pretty rose with the most charming slender pink buds, which open to semi-double rose pink flowers about 3½in (9cm) across with a boss of yellow stamens. The stage at which the outer petals are reflexed and the inner remain cupped is very distinct, and the scent is excellent. Shrub to 7ft (2m) tall. The raiser of this rose is not known, but it appeared in Holland in the late 18th century. Good scent.

'Mme Legras de St Germain' This Alba will grow to 17ft (5m) if trained on a support, but usually makes a shrub around 7ft (2m). Flowers double, well scented, yellowish in the centre when first open. This is possibly a hybrid with a Damask or even a Noisette, as suggested by the yellow colour. Known since 1848.

'Félicité Parmentier' One of the shorter Albas with stems to 4ft (1.2m) and upright flowers. Flowers opening pale pink and reflexing when open. Leaves less blue than most Albas. Presumably raised in France and known since 1834. Good scent.

'Mme Plantier' A tall-growing shrub, which I have seen at Sissinghurst trained to climb into an old apple tree. Flowers double, at first cream, later white, from pretty red-tinted buds. Raised in France in 1835 by M. Plantier, possibly by crossing an Alba with a Noisette. Good scent.

'Céleste'

'Mme Plantier'

'Céleste', an informal shrub for the transition from garden to farmland

'Mme Plantier' on the stump of an old apple tree in the orchard at Sissinghurst

'Tuscany Superb'

Ancient Gallicas

Gallica Roses are usually short, with rather floppy branches and rich red flowers. Their superb scent and intense colour made them one of the most popular flowers in medieval gardens. 'Officinalis' was almost certainly grown by the Romans, and is probably the red rose painted on one of the surviving murals in Pompeii. It is said to have been brought to France from Damascus in the 13th century by Thiebault IV, author of *Le Roman de la Rose*. It was the red rose of Provins which was much cultivated in France for its medicinal properties and perfume. There are good representations of it in medieval paintings, notably in the great altarpiece in Ghent Cathedral, painted in Italy around 1430.

Gallicas are now thought of as typical Old Roses, with very double, flat flowers in rich tones of red and purple. They flower only at midsummer, but are tough and very hardy. The wild *Rosa gallica* is a low suckering shrub with deep pink flowers, found in France eastwards to Russia, growing in heavy, limy soil, and requires water in spring. The garden varieties need this rich soil and will then grow and sucker freely, but they do not thrive in poor light soils on their own roots. Their thin and often floppy shoots need supporting. Budded plants bought from a nursery would probably do better in such poor conditions and the plants would not then form suckers.

PLANTING & PRUNING HELP All roses are best planted from bare root plants in winter. Do not be afraid to cut back the roots of roses to 8in (20cm) or even 6in (15cm) long. They sprout vigorously from the cut ends, so the roots are best kept short and straight, not coiled around in the planting hole. The garden value of once-flowering roses can be extended by planting a delicate clematis or other annual climber to scramble over them to begin flowering after the roses have finished. Gallicas do not need pruning every year, but can be tidied and their supports checked, so that they produce a graceful cascade. If necessary, all shoots can be pruned back to about 3½ft (1m) tall every winter, and the plants kept dwarf. Hardy to −30°F (−35°C), US zones 4–8.

'Rosa Mundi', *Rosa gallica* 'Versicolor', *R. gallica* 'Variegata' This is the striped form of 'Officinalis' and often reverts to plain red. Easily grown and very free-flowering over a long period in midsummer. A shrub up to 3½ft (1m). Good scent.

'Charles de Mills'

'Rosa Mundi'

'Charles de Mills', 'Charles Wills'   A superb rose of German origin with flat flowers of deep reddish purple, fully double and quartered with a light scent. Stems generally to 5ft (1.5m), but can be trained to 7ft (2m) or more on a trellis, where the huge hanging flowers to 3½in (9cm) across can be seen to advantage.

'The Apothecary's Rose', *Rosa gallica* 'Officinalis'   A spreading shrub to 5ft (1.5m) with large semi-double red flowers, fading to purplish that are produced only in midsummer. Leaves green, with fine teeth and a rough upper surface, usually bent down somewhat from the midrib. This is the typical form of the Gallica leaf and can be used to recognize the group. Flowers with some twisted inner petals and numerous yellow stamens. Good scent.

'Tuscany Superb'   One of the deepest coloured Old Roses, known since 1837. Flowers almost double with little scent. The older variety 'Tuscany' has similar smaller flowers. An open shrub to 4ft (1.2m).

'The Apothecary's Rose', *Rosa gallica* 'Officinalis'

'Président de Sèze', a fine specimen at Mottisfont

'Agathe Royale' A large-flowered rose with mid-pink, fully double flowers. This is said to be a hybrid with *Rosa majalis*, a wild rose from northern Europe, and has softer leaves than a pure Gallica. The arching stems are up to 5½ft (1.6m) long. Good scent. Godefroy in 1817.

'Agathe Royale'

'Duc de Guiche', 'Senateur Romain' Flowers large, well-scented and veined with purple in hot weather. Opening crimson, cup-shaped and becoming flat and fully double, showing a green eye. Stems to 5½ft (1.6m), arching. Raised by Prévost in 1829.

'Duchesse d'Angoulême' A lovely rose, pale for a Gallica, with thin, almost translucent petals of the most delicate blush pink. The flowers are heavy for the floppy stems and the plant needs careful support, but is so beautiful that the extra trouble is well taken. Possibly a hybrid with an Alba or a Centifolia, raised by Vibert in France before 1827. A shrub to 3½ft (1m). Good scent.

'L'Impératrice Joséphine' Close to 'Agathe Royale' but with lovelier flowers with pale edges and a deeper centre. The leaves are characteristic, with the ribs impressed and broad wavy stipules. The flowers often fail to open in wet weather in cooler climates, but in warm areas it is a most beautiful rose. It makes an open shrub to 5ft (1.5m). Some scent.

GALLICA ROSES

'Duc de Guiche'

'Duc de Guiche' in the Old Rose garden at
Malmaison near Paris

'Président de Sèze', 'Mme Hébert'   Many of
the best characteristics of the Old Roses are
combined in this lovely flower. It is flat and fully
double with a swirl of petals and often a hint of a
green eye. Colour varies with temperature and
includes shades of pink, violet, magenta and
almost grey, always darker in the centre. The
leaves and strong scent are typical of a Gallica.
Raised in France by Hébert in 1836. 'Jenny Duval'
is now thought to be the same rose, though the
name is older. A shrub to 5ft (1.5m).

'Duchesse d'Angoulême'

'Président de Sèze'

'L'Impératrice Joséphine'

'Perle des Panachées'

such as Vibert and Laffay producing hundreds of new roses of all types. The famous flower painter P. J. Redouté, originally commissioned by Joséphine, continued to publish his great work *Les Roses*, which was eventually completed in 1830.

'Cramoisi Picotée'   A Gallica raised by Vibert in 1834. Flowers crimson with a paler edge, very double, the outer petals reflexed when fully open. Upright stems to 5ft (1.5m); little scent. Not to be confused with 'Cramoisi Supérieur', which is a China, like an improved 'Semperflorens'. An upright plant, nearly 3½ft (1m) tall.

Variegated Gallicas

Gallica roses were developed to their highest expression in the early 19th century in France, where the craze for roses was encouraged by the interest of the Empress Joséphine who had her own collection at Malmaison, on the outskirts of Paris. France's supremacy in rose breeding continued after her death in 1814, with raisers

'Tricolor de Flandres'

'Perle des Panachées'   A Gallica raised by Vibert in 1845. Plant short. Flowers pale pink, lightly variegated with reddish purple. A shrub to 3½ft (1m). Good scent.

'Tricolor de Flandres'   A Gallica raised by Van Houtte in 1846. Flowers large, very pale pink, heavily variegated with red, fading to purple. Plant dense and floppy to 3½ft (1m). Scent good.

'George Vibert'
A Gallica raised by Robert in 1853. Flowers rather small, opening deep pink, fading to pale pink with deeper stripes. Upright stems to 5ft (1.5m). Leaves rather small. Some scent.

'George Vibert'

'Tricolor de Flandres'

A hedge of variegated Gallicas at Hidcote Manor, Gloustershire

'Cramoisi Picotée'

'Tour de Malakoff' leaning over a dwarf box hedge

Gallica Hybrids

Gallica Hybrids are similar in general appearance to pure Gallicas but show signs of the influence of other species in their ancestry. Hardy to −30°F (−35°C), US zones 4–8.

'Burgundiaca', 'Parvifolia', 'Burgundy Rose', 'Pompom de Bourgogne' Sometimes said to be a dwarf sport of Centifolia but close to pure *Rosa gallica*. It has small leaves with narrow leaflets and small reddish pink flowers produced only in summer. It needs full sun and rich soil to flower well and makes a suckering clump of thin stems to 20in (50cm) tall. This rose bears very little resemblance to the true Centifolia and was first recorded in 1664. Some scent.

'Cardinal de Richelieu' A hybrid between a Gallica and a China raised by Laffay in 1840. Flowers opening reddish purple becoming dark purplish with a paler centre to the petals and often with a green eye. The stems reach 5½ft (1.6m) in good conditions, with few thorns. The darkening of the flowers as they age is a characteristic of the China roses. Good scent.

'Tour de Malakoff' Raised by Soupert et Notting in Luxembourg in 1856. Probably a cross between a Gallica and a China or Tea. Flowers very large, opening deep purplish-pink and fading to greyish mauve. Stems to 7½ft (2.3m) with lax shoots which need supporting or can be trained on a pillar. Good scent.

'Cardinal de Richelieu'

GALLICA ROSES

'Ipsilante'

'Ipsilante' Intermediate between a Gallica and a Centifolia with large, medium-pink flowers which open flat. The leaflets are wide, rugose. Plant to 4½ft (1.3m); later-flowering than most

Gallicas and reported by David Austin to be particularly disease-resistant. Scent good.

'Complicata' A large shrub around 7ft (2m) or a climber to 10ft (3m) if trained into a tree or on a wall. Flowers large, single, pink with a paler centre. This can create a wonderful effect, like a superb Dog rose, and indeed 'Complicata' is possibly a hybrid between *Rosa gallica* and one of the wild Dog roses, or, as Fred Boutin has suggested, with the American *Rosa setigera*. Good scent, derived from *Rosa gallica*.

'de la Grifferaie' A hybrid between a Gallica and possibly *Rosa multiflora* raised by Vibert in 1846. Flowers in clusters, deep pink fading to purple, with a good rich scent. Stems to 7ft (2m) with few thorns. 'Russelliana' is similar but is very thorny. Both these roses are very tough and are said to have been used as understocks. They are sometimes found wild in hedges and in old gardens but are worth growing for their own good points. Scent good.

'Complicata'

'de la Grifferaie'

'Complicata'

'Burgundiaca'

19

Damask Roses

The Damask roses are another ancient group, probably grown in the Greek colonies in Asia Minor for their beauty and for their essential oil which can be extracted and distilled to make Attar of Roses. In parts of Turkey around Isparta, the dusty volcanic hillsides are planted with the Damask rose 'Trigintipetala', the flowers of which are harvested before sunrise every morning, and sent to the distillary.

The origins of the Damask roses are uncertain, but they are thought to be hybrids between *Rosa gallica* and the wild Musk rose of southern Turkey, *Rosa phoenicia*. The so-called Autumn Damask, which flowers in autumn as well as summer, is thought to have arisen from *Rosa gallica* and the autumn-flowering *Rosa moschata*, a mysterious rose which has never been found wild.

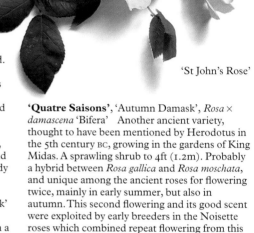

'St John's Rose'

PLANTING & PRUNING HELP   Damasks need much the same treatment as Gallicas; they need little pruning other than cutting off the dead flowering shoots and encouraging the new summer shoots. In the taller varieties these new shoots can be pegged down to make a low shrub, or trained on a fence. Hard pruning to the ground after flowering will rejuvenate a leggy plant. Hardy to −20°F (−29°C), US zones 5–9.

***Rosa × damascena* 'Trigintipetala'**, 'Kazanlik' An ancient Damask forming an upright bush to 7ft (2m); its flowers are rather loose doubles with a wonderful scent. In places where it is grown for rose oil to make scent, the plants are pruned with shears to around 3½ft (1m) high after flowering, and every five years or so, cut to the ground! An ancient variety of unrecorded origin, but possibly *Rosa gallica* 'Officinalis' × *Rosa phoenicia*.

***Rosa × damascena* 'Versicolor'**, 'York and Lancaster' A Damask known since 1551 with flowers of unstable colour, some palest pink, some deeper and some showing both colours. Similar in habit to 'Trigintipetala' and probably a sport from it. Makes a lax shrub to 5ft (1.5m). Good scent.

'St John's Rose', *Rosa sancta*, *R. × richardii*, 'The Holy Rose' An ancient form of Damask rose with single, pale pink flowers on a rounded bush to 5ft (1.5m) tall. This rose has been identified from the remains of a floral chaplet found in an Egyptian tomb dating from the Roman period, and is now grown around churches in Ethiopia, from whence it was introduced to Europe in 1895. Scent slight.

'Quatre Saisons', 'Autumn Damask', *Rosa × damascena* 'Bifera'   Another ancient variety, thought to have been mentioned by Herodotus in the 5th century BC, growing in the gardens of King Midas. A sprawling shrub to 4ft (1.2m). Probably a hybrid between *Rosa gallica* and *Rosa moschata*, and unique among the ancient roses for flowering twice, mainly in early summer, but also in autumn. This second flowering and its good scent were exploited by early breeders in the Noisette roses which combined repeat flowering from this and from old Chinese garden roses. 'Quatre Saisons' also sported to produce the white Moss rose 'Quatre Saisons Blanche Mousseuse'.

Rosa × damascena 'Versicolor'

DAMASK ROSES

Rosa × damascena 'Trigintipetala' growing for the Attar of Roses perfume in Turkey

'Quatre Saisons'

'Omar Khayyám'

Damask Roses

In the minds of Europeans, Damask roses were associated with the Saracens who cultivated these roses in the Dark Ages. 'Damascena', from Damascus alludes to their origin, and some of the later varieties were introduced from Persia where they continued to be grown. There, roses were associated with Sufism, a mystical philosophy in which they symbolized understanding and union with God.

'Ispahan'

'Celsiana'   A Damask known since 1732, with attractive, semi-double flowers which open deepish pink and cupped before fading to almost white. An upright bush to 5ft (1.5m) tall with greyish green leaves. Good scent.

'Ispahan', 'Pompom des Princes'   A Damask known since 1832, whose association with the city of Ispahan is not recorded. Flowers rich pink, very double with a very good scent, freely produced in the latter part of the Old Rose season, on a rather tall shrub to 7ft (2m). This rose is extremely tolerant of shade; even in very deep shade it will not show evidence of mildew.

'Omar Khayyám'   An untidy rose with a romantic past that grows to about 3½ft (1m). When William Simpson, an artist with *The Illustrated London News* visited the tomb of Omar Khayyám in Nashaipur in NE Iran, he collected seeds of the rose which grew over the astronomer poet's grave. These were raised at Kew and first flowered in 1894. One was planted on the grave of Edward Fitzgerald, translator of the *Rubaiyat*, in Boulge churchyard in Suffolk by a group of his friends and admirers. It is an upright shrub, with untidy double flowers but an excellent scent.

'Celsiana'

'Omar Khayyám'

'Celsiana' with *Campanula alliarifolia* at Mottisfont

Pale Damasks

Because of the white-flowered climbing roses in their ancestry, Damask roses have a wider range of colours than Gallicas, and there are many more in pale pinks or white. These include some of the most delicately beautiful of Old Roses. The climbing ancestry also tends to produce long summer shoots in the more robust varieties. These shoots can be shortened to the required length in winter, but flowers will be produced all along them if they are pegged down or trained horizontally in winter or early spring. Hardy to −20°F (−29°C), US zones 5–9.

'Hebe's Lip'

'Blush Damask' This rose has some of the characters of a Scotch rose as well as a Damask, with rather rounded leaflets and smallish but well-scented flowers. The whole bush is twiggy and prickly with stems to 7ft (2m) tall. If grown on its own roots, this suckers freely like the Scotch rose. Of unrecorded origin. Good scent.

'Duchesse de Montebello' A robust, tall shrub to 5½ft (1.6m), with lush, greyish, broad leaflets and upright heads of smallish neat flowers with a good scent. Colour described as pale coral with crimson streaks on the bud, fading to palest pink after opening fully. Raised by Laffay before 1829, and possibly a backcross between Autumn Damask or a China, and a Gallica. Maréchal Lannes, later Duc de Montebello, was one of Napoléon's generals.

'Hebe's Lip', 'Rubrotincta', 'Reine Blanche'
In this almost single rose the creamy flowers are edged crimson in the bud, and the tinting remains in the open flower. The shoots and twigs are very thorny with recurved thorns and the flowers are in a branched head. Height about 5½ft (1.6m). Raised in England by William Paul of Waltham Cross in 1912, probably by crossing a Damask with a Sweetbriar. Good scent.

'Blanchefleur'

'Duchesse de Montebello' at the Royal National Rose Society's garden at St Albans

'Duchesse de Montebello'

'Leda'

'Blush Damask'

'Leda', 'Painted Damask'   A lovely rose with a dense double, quartered flower with white petals edged red from a red bud. It makes a low bush around 3½ft (1m) tall with rather rounded, lush, dark green leaflets. A few flowers are sometimes produced in the autumn as well. An old variety known since 1827. Good scent.

'Blanchefleur'   A Damask raised by Vibert at Angers, France in 1835. Shoots spiny, to 7ft (2m) or more, usually with rather pale green leaves. Flowers medium-sized, opening palest pink, fading to white, very sweetly scented.

'Mme Hardy'

'La Ville de Bruxelles'

Damask Roses

Damask roses were very popular in France from the 17th century until the mid-19th century when breeders found improvements harder and harder to achieve, and became more excited by Moss roses partly derived from *Rosa × centifolia* and by hybrids raised from newly introduced Chinese repeat-flowering roses which led to the Bourbons, Hybrid Perpetuals and Hybrid Teas. Hardy to −20°F (−29°C), US zones 5–9.

'La Ville de Bruxelles' One of the largest flowered and most richly coloured of the Damasks with fully double, flat flowers with a good scent. It forms a very leafy bush with stems to 5½ft (1.6m). Raised by Vibert of Angers in 1849. An altogether fine rose.

'Mme Zöetmans' One of the smaller Damasks which forms a lax bush to 4½ft (1.3m) tall. The leaves are bright green and the neat flowers with a pink flush on opening, fading to white, often showing a green eye. Raised by Marest in France in 1830. Good scent.

'Mme Hardy' A Damask possibly crossed with an Alba, raised by M. Eugene Hardy, curator of the Luxembourg Gardens in Paris in 1832.

'Petite Lisette'

DAMASK ROSES

'Mme Zöetmans' showing hazel staves used to support the arching stems

A classic Old Rose with pure white flowers and a green eye, opening flat. A strong grower producing shoots to 7ft (2m) or more in summer, which benefit from being trained horizontally or pegged down to flower all along their length. Good scent.

'Oeillet Parfait' A small-growing Damask with stems up to 4½ft (1.3m) and lush green leaves. Flowers quite large, rich pink, fully double, opening flat and almost reflexing. Raised by Foulard in 1841. *Oeillet* is carnation in French. Some fragrance.

'Petite Lisette' A small-flowered Damask raised by Vibert of Angers in 1817. Flowers with a rich scent, pink, perfectly double with petals shorter than the green tips of the sepals. Shoots very thorny, with slightly greyish leaves, on a bushy plant to 4½ft (1.3m).

'Oeillet Parfait'

Rosa × centifolia

'Petite de Hollande'

Centifolia Roses

Rosa × centifolia, also called the Cabbage rose, is an ancient hybrid between 'Quatre Saisons', the Autumn Damask and a form of Alba. The first Centifolias are recorded around the end of the 16th century, and are commonly seen in 17th-century Dutch flower paintings as large, double, pale pink roses. The original Centifolia is sterile and most other Centifolias are sports or mutants from the original. Only after the early 19th century were some varieties raised from seed. Moss roses appeared in this group as well as in Damasks. Centifolias make rather floppy shrubs and flower only in early summer, but their flowers are beautiful and the scent is excellent.

PLANTING & PRUNING HELP   Feed well and prune after flowering; shorten long shoots, peg down or tie in winter. Hardy to−20°F (−29°C), US zones 5–9.

***Rosa × centifolia*, 'Old Cabbage Rose'**   A rose with lovely double, rich pink flowers from fat buds, produced singly or in bunches, weighing down the stems. The outer petals curl back, but their only failing is a tendency to ball in wet weather. The leaves are lush with broad leaflets and coarse teeth. The stems reach 5½ft (1.6m) but need supporting on a low fence or with a triangle of stakes. Good scent.

***Rosa × centifolia* 'Variegata'**, 'Village Maid', 'Belle des Jardins'   A mutant of Centifolia with variegated pink and white flowers, introduced at Angers, a great centre of rose breeding, in 1845. It makes a strong thorny bush to 7ft (2m) but may revert to the ordinary pink. The flowers are easily spoiled by rain. Good scent.

Rosa × centifolia
'Variegata'

CENTIFOLIA ROSES

'Bullata'

'Bullata' 'Rose à Feuilles de Laitue'
A sport of Centifolia first recorded in 1801, with
lush curled and puckered leaves, reddish when
young, and the usual large pink flowers, very
double and cupped when they are at their perfect
stage. The extra large leaves mean that it also
needs careful supporting if it is to look graceful
without collapsing. Grows to 5ft (1.5m) tall.
Good scent.

'Petite de Hollande', 'Pompom des Dames'
A small Centifolia with well-scented, fully
double flowers, sometimes with pale edges
and a deeper centre, on a bush about
3½ft (1m) high. A very good and free-
flowering dwarf which originated in
Holland around 1800. Good scent.

'Unique Blanche', 'White Provence Unique'
This lovely delicate rose is a sport of Centifolia
discovered at Needham in Suffolk in 1775. The
buds are greenish, tipped with red. The flowers
open creamy, fading to pure white with thin-
textured petals. One of the later flowering Old
Roses. The leaves are the usual Centifolia type
with broad blunt teeth. A sprawling shrub to 5ft
(1.5m). Good scent.

'Unique Blanche'

29

The Old Rose Garden at the Roseraie de l'Haÿ-les-Roses, near Orly, Paris

'Shailer's White Moss'

Rosa × *centifolia* 'Muscosa'

'Cristata'

Centifolia Moss Roses

Moss roses first appeared as sports or mutants of *Rosa × centifolia* in the late 17th century. The twigs and the sepals are covered with dense masses of sticky glands which are scented like the leaves of the Eglantine rose. All the roses on this page appeared as sports of *Rosa × centifolia* and have typical Centifolia-like flowers.

'Cristata'

PLANTING & PRUNING HELP   As with all Old roses, feed well and prune after flowering; in winter, shorten long shoots, peg down or tie in. Hardy to −20°F (−29°C), US zones 5–9.

Rosa × centifolia **'Muscosa'**, 'Old Moss Rose', 'Common Moss'   This, the original mossy sport of Centifolia was recorded in the late 17th century. The flowers and leaves are the same as the common Centifolia, and the stems and sepals are well covered in moss. It flowers once, but over a long season of about two months in England, mostly after midsummer. A large sprawling shrub to 6ft (1.8m). Excellent scent.

'Cristata', 'Chapeau de Napoléon', 'Crested Moss'   This mutant is halfway to a Moss, with feathery outgrowths only on the edges of the sepals. It was noticed on the wall of an old convent in Fribourg, in Switzerland around 1820, and was introduced to cultivation by Vibert in 1826. The upright stems can reach 5ft (1.5m) and the leaves are typical of Centifolia. Good scent.

'Shailer's White Moss', 'Centifolia Muscosa Alba', 'White Bath'   This white sport of the Common Moss, *Rosa × centifolia* 'Muscosa', appeared in 1788. It makes a loose bush to 5ft (1.5m), with the same shaped flowers as its parent, usually all white, though sometimes one appears that partially reverts to pink. The flowers often show a green button eye. Good scent.

'Comtesse de Murinais'

Damask Moss Roses

Damask Moss roses first appeared in 1835. In the mid-19th century Moss roses enjoyed a vogue, and many different varieties were raised, especially in France. Some of them had China roses in their ancestry, so that reliable repeat-flowering Mosses were produced, combining the repeating of the Autumn Damask and the China. One of these, the tall-growing, bluish purple 'William Lobb', raised in 1855 is still popular.

PLANTING & PRUNING HELP Damask Mosses need much the same treatment as Damasks; they need little pruning other than cutting off the dead flowering shoots and encouraging the new summer shoots. In the taller varieties these new shoots can be pegged down to make a low shrub, or trained on a fence or a pillar. Hardy to −20°F (−29°C), US zones 5–9.

'Quatre Saisons Blanche Mousseuse', 'Bifera Alba Muscosa', 'Perpetual White Moss' A white mossy mutant of the Autumn Damask which often reverts to the plain pink 'Quatre Saisons'. An upright bush to 5½ft (1.6m) with medium-sized white flowers and very mossy buds, long narrow sepals and flower stalks. The flowers are well scented and are produced mainly in summer, with a few extra flowers into autumn. The leaves are pale green with fine teeth. This sport was first recorded in 1835. Good scent.

'Capitaine John Ingram'
A dark-flowered Mossy Damask, raised by Laffay in 1854. Close to 'Nuits de Young', but with neater reflexing petals of slightly richer colour, opening crimson, becoming purple. Leaflets broad with impressed veins. A shrub to 4ft (1.2m). The moss on the stalks and buds is rather thin. Good scent.

'Capitaine John Ingram'

'Baron de Wassenaer' A lovely rose with cupped flowers of rich pink, produced in large bunches over a long period. The flower shape suggests that one parent may have been a Bourbon. It was raised by Verdier in 1854, a time when Bourbons were very popular. The bushes are upright, to 4½ft (1.3m), gracefully arching under the weight of flowers. The moss is brownish, the leaves with broad leaflets. Good scent.

'Comtesse de Murinais' One of the tallest growing of the Mosses, with tall shoots to 8ft (2.5m). Flowers medium-sized, opening palest pink, fading to white and well scented as is the moss. Raised by Vibert in 1843. Good scent, but rather subject to mildew.

'Nuits de Young'
A Damask Moss with very dark purple flowers raised by Laffay in 1845. The leaves are small and dark, the flowers medium-sized, among the darkest of all Old Roses, as dark as the ancient Gallicas, and showing some stamens when fully open. Plant suckering, upright, to 5ft (1.5m). Good scent.

'Nuits de Young'

'Quatre Saisons Blanche Mousseuse' showing pink flowers where it has reverted to 'Quatre Saisons'

'Baron de Wassenaer'

DAMASK MOSSES

'James Mitchell'

'Blanche Moreau'

'Henri Martin'

'Striped Moss'

'Blanche Moreau'   A Mossy Damask with sweetly scented white flowers with a pale flesh-pink flush. Leaves dark green. Stems strong to 7ft (2m) with purplish moss. Most of the flowering is in summer, but a few flowers are produced later in the year; this repeat flowering comes from the parent, 'Quatre Saisons Blanche Mousseuse', which was crossed with 'Comtesse de Murinais', a tall-growing white Moss. Introduced by Moreau-Robert of Angers in 1880. Good scent.

'Général Kléber'   A Mossy Damask hybrid, probably with a Bourbon such as 'Souvenir de Malmaison'; has large, pale pink, flat flowers with good scent. The moss is green and the leaves have broad leaflets and stipules. A strong, bushy upright shrub to 5½ft (1.6m) raised by Robert in 1856. Général Kléber was Napoleon's commander in Egypt and was assassinated in Cairo in 1800.

'Henri Martin'   A Mossy Damask raised by Laffay in 1863. The flowers are a good red, semi-double on a tall shrub to 7ft (2m). The slender stalks are well covered in long thin moss. Said to do well on a north wall. Good scent.

'James Mitchell'   A Mossy Damask raised by Verdier in 1861. The moss is brownish and the very double, deep pink flowers are well scented. A rather short plant, to 4ft (1.2m), and very free-flowering. Good scent.

'Striped Moss', 'Oeillet Panaché'   A Mossy Damask with striped flowers of pale pink, streaked with deep pink. The leaflets are rather narrow, the flowers medium-sized. A small shrub to just under 3½ft (1m), ideal for a large pot or tub. Raised by Du Pont in 1880. Some scent.

DAMASK MOSSES

'Général Kléber' with white foxgloves at Mottisfont

'Little Gem'   A miniature Damask Moss with deep pink flowers on a small bush up to 3½ft (1m) high. An English variety raised by Paul in 1880. The flowers are stiffly upright, of good shape; the moss is rather thin. Good scent.

'Little Gem'

'Little Gem'

'Louis Gimard'

Mosses of Mixed Parentage

Most of the Moss roses only flower once in spite of the Autumn Damask parentage that many of them possess. In a few, however, repeat-flowering is preserved, and these can be relied on to flower in autumn as well as summer. Many of these repeat-flowering Mosses, and some of the once-flowering ones, have flowers closer to the Bourbons (which were being raised at the same time), than to pure Damasks and are probably Bourbon-Damask hybrides. As the Bourbon rose was already a cross between an Autumn Damask and a China rose, these roses were three-quarters Damask to a quarter China.

PLANTING & PRUNING HELP

To encourage a good crop of late flowers, fertilize and water the roses well after the first crop of flowers has finished. Where dead flowers have been cut from the branching heads, it is necessary to remove the whole head and reduce the old flowering shoots by three or four leaves, down to a strong dormant bud. It is from this bud that the second crop of flowering shoots will emerge. Hardy to −20°F (−29°C), US zones 5–9.

'Gloire des Mousseux' A Moss with a large pink flower, of Bourbon rather than Damask shape, raised by Laffay in 1852. It makes a stiff, upright bushy plant to 4½ft (1.3m). The sweetly scented flowers are produced mainly in summer, with a few late ones appearing in autumn. Good scent.

'Louis Gimard' A Mossy Damask-China cross, raised by Pernet (*père*) in 1877. It makes a low bush around 5ft (1.5m) tall, with dark green leaves. The flowers are well scented, purplish pink with a crimson centre on opening. Some scent.

'Soupert et Notting'

'Soupert et Notting' An almost perpetual flowering Mossy Damask with a Bourbon-like flower. A short plant to 4ft (1.2m). The buds and flower stalks are densely covered in green moss. The flowers are a good pink with a deeper centre and well scented. This is one of the best of all the Moss roses, raised by Pernet in 1874, and named after Soupert et Notting, a nursery in Luxumbourg. Good scent.

'William Lobb', 'Old Velvet Moss' A tall shrub, throwing up long canes to over 7ft (2m). The flowers are formed in bunches and are purplish

'William Lobb'

MOSS ROSES

'William Lobb' at the back of a border in the kitchen garden at Hidcote

crimson on opening, fading to purple and then almost grey. This rose often survives in old gardens and is very tough. Like 'Comtesse de Murinais' it is suitable for the back of a border or for training up some support. Raised by Laffay in 1855. Although this is also a Bourbon cross, it flowers only once. Good scent.

'Gloire des Mousseux'

'Salet'

'Salet' This is one of the most reliable repeat-flowering Moss roses. It is a large Damask with strong shoots reaching 5½ft (1.6m), with large leaves and rather narrow leaflets. Unfortunately, the flowers, though well scented are rather untidy, pale pink with a muddled centre. Raised in France by Lacharme in 1854. Good scent.

'Comte de Chambord'   'Jacques Cartier'

Portland Roses

Portland roses were named after Margaret Cavendish Bentinck, 2nd Duchess of Portland, who grew them in her garden in 1800. The original Portland rose (*shown here*) was recorded in 1792. It is a good red and valued for its late flowering. Later, other similar crosses came to be grouped with the Portlands and extended the colour range of this small group. However, from 1816 onwards, when crossed with Chinas again,

they were overshadowed by their progeny, the Hybrid Perpetuals , which were the largest and most important group of roses until the arrival of the Hybrid Teas.

PLANTING & PRUNING HELP   Portland roses are best planted from bare root plants in winter. Cut back the roots to 8in (20cm) or even 6in (15cm); they sprout vigorously from the cut ends so the roots are best kept short and straight, not coiled around in the planting hole. Portlands do not need pruning every year, but can be tidied and their supports checked. If necessary, all shoots can be pruned back to about 2ft (60cm) every winter and the plants kept dwarf. Hardy to −20°F (−29°C), US zones 5–9.

'Comte de Chambord'   A lovely rose with characteristic Old Rose flowers; very large, flat, fully double and filled with a swirl of petals. It is a good repeat-flowerer, the later flowers coming in flushes according to the weather. Shoots upright, to 5ft (1.5m). Flowers purplish pink, thin petalled but well scented. This is said to be a Portland crossed with a China, which strictly means that it should be grouped with the Hybrid Perpetuals, but because of its flower shape is usually put with Portlands. Raised by Moreau-Robert in 1860. Good scent.

'Portland Rose'   The original Portland rose is a low suckering shrub to 2½ft (75cm) tall with bright red, semi-double, well-scented flowers produced both in summer and autumn. It was first

'Rose de Resht'

PORTLAND ROSES

'Rose de Resht'

'Portland Rose' at Mottisfont

'Rose du Roi'

recorded in 1782 and its origin is something of a mystery. It is said to have been obtained from Italy by the Duchess. Its parentage was guessed to be Autumn Damask × *Rosa gallica* 'Officinalis', and it is certainly very close to the Gallica parent. However, a rose with this parentage would be unlikely to flower a second time, so its has been suggested that a red China rose may be in its ancestry too.

'Jacques Cartier' A good rose, also a Portland crossed with a China, raised by Moreau-Robert in 1868. A low shrub to 4½ft (1.3m) with flat, fully double flowers with a button eye. Good scent.

'Rose de Resht' A thorny upright shrub to 5ft (1.5m) tall, with well-scented flat flowers close to the leaves. This rose was introduced into cultivation in 1950 by Nancy Lindsay, the friend and heiress of Lawrence Johnston, creator of the famous gardens at Hidcote and Serra de la Madone at Menton. In later life she grew and sold Old Roses, and described its discovery in her list: 'Happened on it in an old Persian garden in ancient Resht, tribute of the tea caravans plodding Persia-wards from China over the Central Asian

Steppes; it is a sturdy yard-high bush of glazed lizard green, perpetually emblazoned with full camellia flowers of pigeon's blood ruby, irised with royal purple, haloed with dragon sepals like the painted blooms on Oriental faience.' Her allusion to China is not too far-fetched, as there is evidence that Damask roses found their way to China before the 18th century, and this rose may be an ancient Damask-China cross. Good scent.

'Rose du Roi', 'Lee's Crimson Perpetual'
A small shrub with good red flowers, sometimes marked with purple. Repeat-flowering and well scented, it makes a low shrub to 2½ft (75cm) tall. This rose is important in rose ancestry as it was the source of the good red colour and good scent which came into modern roses via the Hybrid Perpetuals. Good scent.

Climbing 'Souvenir de la Malmaison' on an old wall

Bourbon Roses

Bourbon roses are named after l'Ile de Bourbon, now the island of Réunion near Mauritius in the Indian Ocean. In the days before the Suez Canal was opened, this was an important port of call for French ships returning from the Far East. Apparently, both the Autumn Damask and the China 'Old Blush' were planted in hedges there and their hybrid was found and taken into local gardens. From Réunion, seeds were sent to Paris, where they were grown by M. Jacques, gardener to Louis Philippe, and named 'Rosier de l'Ile de Bourbon'. This first Bourbon was introduced in 1823, but is now very seldom seen, though it was a reliable autumn-flowerer with a wonderful scent.

When crossed with other Tea and China roses, it contributed to a new group of roses, often tall, with good scent and usually autumn- as well as summer-flowering.

PLANTING & PRUNING HELP These Bourbon climbers should be pruned like Ramblers, in autumn or winter. The old shoots which have flowered, can be cut away completely, and the long new shoots tied down, as arches or along a low fence. If this seems too drastic, feed the plants well and tidy up last summer's flowering

'Prince Charles'

'Blairii No. 2'

BOURBON ROSES

branches. Remove them completely the following year when strong new shoots should have formed. Hardy to −20°F (−29°C), US zones 5–9.

'Blairii No. 2' This climbing Bourbon has some of the loveliest flowers among the Old Roses. They are perfectly round, pale pink, deeper in the centre, with a good scent. The stems can reach 17ft (5m), and can be trained on a tree or a pergola. Flowering is mainly in midsummer, but a few later flowers can appear in a good season; well scented. I have often admired this rose but have never grown it; it is said to get mildew. Raised in England by a Mr Blair in 1845. 'Blairii No. 1' is similar but has paler flowers and is shorter, growing to 7ft (2m).

'Great Western' A Bourbon raised by Laffay in 1838 and with an an unusual name for a French rose. It is once-flowering only in midsummer. Flowers large, purplish pink, fully double; leaflets broad. Stems to 5ft (1.5m). Good scent.

'Prince Charles' Once-flowering, with well-scented reddish flowers which fade to lilac. An arching shrub with stems 5ft (1.5m) long. A Bourbon of unknown origin, first recorded in 1842. Good scent.

'Souvenir de la Malmaison' A large-flowered rose with flat flowers of palest pink, named in remembrance of Josephine's garden. Although she died in 1814, the garden continued to be looked after until it was finally sold in 1824. The flowers are filled with small petals with a shadow of deeper pink in the centre. Raised by Beluze in 1843 by crossing 'Mme Desprez', a Bourbon, with a Tea

'Bourbon Queen'

rose. Reliably repeat-flowering and well scented. Its white sport, 'Kronprinzessin Victoria' has a creamy centre. The semi-double sport, 'Souvenir de St Anne's' is illustrated below. There is also an excellent climbing form which I have found surviving in old gardens. Inclined to ball in wet weather; it grows to 6ft (1.8m) but up to 12ft (3.5m) in the climbing form. Good scent.

'Bourbon Queen', 'Queen of Bourbons', 'Reine des Îles Bourbon' This rampant rose is a survivor often found in old gardens, clothing a fence or growing out of a hedge. It is disappointing among Bourbons because it flowers once only, but makes up for that by covering itself with bunches of flowers for a long period in midsummer. The shoots, which are up to 10ft (3m) long, are best tied in horizontally along a fence. The leaflets are unusally broad and the flowers cup-shaped, pink with paler edges and well scented. Raised in France by Mauget in 1834.

'Great Western'

'Bourbon Queen'

Bourbon Roses

Though the earlier Bourbons were often climbers and once-flowering, the later ones were shorter, often medium-sized shrubs which flower continuously through the summer, if given sufficient water, and into autumn. After a dry summer these autumn flowers are particularly welcome, and are often better than those produced in the heat of midsummer.

PLANTING & PRUNING HELP   Plant roses which are susceptible to mildew where the roots get plenty of water and the tops are not in a draught (they will get worse mildew if they are planted under the eaves of a house, or against a wall which faces away from rain-bearing winds). In a cooler, wetter spot, mildew will not be so bad. Blackspot is always worse on weak or half-hidden shoots. Keep the plants well fed and do not leave feeble shoots near the base; they will not flower anyway. Hardy to 0°F (–18°C), US zones 7–10.

'Kathleen Harrop'   A pale-flowered sport of 'Zéphirine Drouhin', introduced by Alexander Dickson in Northern Ireland in 1919. The flowers are loosely double and the reflexing petals have a pale face and deeper reverse. It is also susceptible to mildew. A large shrub or climber to 8ft (2.5m). Good scent.

'La Reine Victoria'   A lovely rose with delicate, cupped and incurved deep rose pink flowers in a loose bunch on upright stems to 7ft (2m). Scent good, and a reliable repeat-flowerer. This and its pale sport, 'Mme Pierre Oger' are the epitome of late Victorian roses. Raised in Lyon by J. Schwartz in 1872. Unfortunately, it does suffer from blackspot.

'Louise Odier', 'Mme de Stella'   The repeat-flowering of the typical Bourbon is shown in this lovely Old Rose, with perfect, flat, fully double,

'Kathleen Harrop'

'La Reine Victoria'

'Mme Lauriol de Barny'

'Mme Pierre Oger'

'Zéphirine Drouhin'

richly scented flowers produced in loose bunches into autumn. Their colour is bluish-pink, shaded with lilac. The stems are strong, reaching 5ft (1.5m). Raised in France by Margottin in 1851. One of the best Old Roses. Some scent.

'Mme Lauriol de Barny' A mid-pink rose with flat, fully double flowers with good scent. Flowers in bunches, mainly in summer, but with a few later. Stems to 7ft (2m) or more. Raised in France by Trouillard in 1868.

'Mme Pierre Oger' This pale sport of 'La Reine Victoria' was found by M. Oger in Caen in 1874 and was introduced by Verdier in 1878. It became even more popular than its parent. Its most delicate, very pale pink petals flush with deeper pink and crimson in hot weather. Stems upright to 7ft (2m). Good scent.

'Zéphirine Drouhin' A very easily recognized rose with almost thornless twigs on a tall shrub or climber to 10ft (3m). The flowers are deep, bright pink, of good scent and loosely double. They are produced throughout summer and autumn, the plant rarely being without flowers. Its only drawback is that it always suffers from mildew which disfigures the leaves. Mildew is worse on plants which are dry at the roots, so this should be planted where the roots are not dry in summer, and fed and watered well. It also suffers from blackspot. Raised in France by Bizot in 1868.

'Louise Odier'

'Variegata di Bologna'

Bourbon Roses

Striped and multicoloured roses have always been popular, from the early Gallica 'Rosa Mundi' to the modern multicoloured giant Hybrid Teas raised in New Zealand by Sam McGredy IV, and the striped Miniatures of Californian Ralf Moore. A group of late 19th-century and early 20th-century ones have survived, valued as much for their freedom of flowering and good scent, as for their colour. Three are Bourbons, the fourth is a Hybrid Perpetual.

By the late 19th century, breeders of roses had moved on from Bourbons and concentrated on Hybrid Perpetuals and Hybrid Teas, and the few later Bourbons are sports from earlier ones, which were preserved by connoisseurs of Old Roses.

'Commandant Beaurepaire'

'Commandant Beaurepaire', 'Panachée d'Angers'   The oldest of four rather similar striped roses, the others being 'Variegata de Bologna', 'Honorine de Brabant' and 'Ferdinand Pichard'. 'Commandant Beaurepaire' has deep pink flowers variegated with red, fading to purple, with little contrast between the two colours; on a dense bush up to 5ft (1.5m). Raised in France by Moreau-Robert in 1874. Some scent.

'Honorine de Brabant'

BOURBON ROSES

'Souvenir de St Anne's'

'Honorine de Brabant' A Bourbon of unknown origin with neat flowers, cup-shaped on opening, produced well into autumn. They have deep pink or purplish stripes and flecks on a pale pink ground, and are not fully double, showing some stamens when fully open. The scent is particularly good. It makes a strong leafy plant, up to 7ft (2m) tall, and may be used to clothe a pillar. 'Ferdinand Pichard' (*not shown*), is similar but the flowers are more heavily marked and more fully double.

'Variegata di Bologna' The most flashy of the old striped roses, with crimson, then purple stripes on an almost white ground, but produced mainly in summer with only the occasional autumn flowering. Raised in Italy in 1909 by Lodi-Bonfiglioli. A strong grower with stems to 8ft (2.5m), which can be arched over to form a lower, wider shrub. Good scent.

'Mme Isaac Pereire' This is one of the largest-flowered of the Old Roses, with flat, very double, flowers around 5in (12cm) across. These open a rich reddish and fade to purplish pink, the outer petals curving under, the centre often quartered, and in spring often showing green proliferation. The leaflets are broad, dark green and overlapping. The stout stems can reach 7½ft (2.3m) , so the plant can be trained as a pillar rose or low climber. Raised in France in 1881 by Garçon. Good scent. Flowers well in autumn.

'Souvenir de St Anne's' A modern Bourbon, found as a sport of 'Souvenir de la Malmaison' in the garden of Lady Ardilaun, at St Anne's, Clontarf, near Dublin, and introduced by Graham Thomas in 1950; it is still one of his favourite roses. While 'Souvenir de la Malmaison' is a very solid, full double, and likely to ball and rot in wet weather, 'Souvenir de St Anne's ' is only semi-double and so is more reliable in wet areas. It makes a tall bush to 7ft (2m), with well-scented flowers both in summer and autumn. Good scent.

'Mme Isaac Pereire'

45

Old China Roses

The introduction of the perpetual-flowering China rose into rose breeding brought repeat flowering into European cultivated roses, and led to the development of the Teas and Hybrid Teas in the 20th century. It was thought that the Chinese had been growing perpetual-flowering garden roses for some time before they were introduced into Europe. This was based on the slender evidence of a painting on silk dating from AD 965, although there is little about roses in ancient Chinese horticultural literature until around the 18th century.

The date of their first introduction to Europe is equally uncertain. Among the 32 roses growing in his garden at Lambeth in 1656, John Tradescant lists *Rosa mensalis*, the monthly rose. A specimen is found in the Herbarium of Gronovius in 1704, but the dates given below, when living plants were brought by ship from Canton, are those generally accepted. These China roses were soon improved upon by breeders in France, and it is mainly because of their great toughness and reliable perpetual flowering that the ones shown here have survived at all.

PLANTING & PRUNING HELP China roses need only a little pruning and the dead wood and old flowering stems tidied away, but thrive on rich feeding and ample warmth and humidity in summer. China roses are not very hardy, normally surviving 0°F (−18°C), US zones 7–10.

Rosa chinensis var. *spontanea* This wild climber is thought to be the most important parent of the cultivated China roses. It grows scattered over a large area in western Sichuan and Hubei, but is never common. The stems reach 13ft (4m) or more when climbing into trees, and in the open it forms a large arching shrub. The leaves are small, evergreen and very hardy. The lightly scented flowers are produced singly in spring only, and where we saw them wild in northwest Sichuan, varied in colour from red to white, often opening pink and becoming dark red before the petals fell. Although recorded by plant collectors such as Augustine Henry at the beginning of the 20th century, this wild rose was only introduced to Europe by Mikinori Ogisu in 1990. It is easy to grow, but needs to be well established in a hot position before it will flower freely. The flowers are produced on the old wood, so the long shoots should be left on until they have flowered.

'Old Blush China', 'Parson's Pink China', 'Monthly Rose' This was definitely brought to Europe from Canton by Peter Osbeck in 1751. It is a hardy, free-flowering shrub and easy to root from cuttings. We have seen it growing in village gardens in western China as well as by old farms in Devon. Around five to ten mid-pink flowers,

'Old Blush China'

'Semperflorens'

'Pompon de Paris'   *Rosa chinensis* var. *spontanea* growing wild in NW Sichuan

which darken as they age, are produced in a branching head. Each flower is about 2½in (6cm) across, with a light scent. The shrub form grows to 4ft (1.2m) and there is also a climbing form. We suspect that this has some Multiflora in its ancestry as *Rosa multiflora* is wild in the same parts of China, where wild double Ramblers are common.

'Semperflorens', 'Slater's Crimson China' Another early introduction to Europe from Chinese gardens, reported in 1792. A dwarf around 1ft (30cm) tall, with deep red flowers flecked with white on slender nodding stalks. This rose is still grown in W China and is long-lived in gardens, although never very strong, needing good cultivation to grow into a decent bush. It is the parent of most of the early deep red roses.

Rosa chinensis **'Viridiflora'** An ugly curiosity, first recorded in 1843 in Europe, but presumably also originating in China. It has no petals, but a tight mass of leafy sepals. It is similar in growth to 'Old Blush' and probably a sport of it.

Rosa chinensis var. *spontanea* from SW Sichuan

'Pompon de Paris' A Miniature rose, now generally seen in its climbing form. It is close to wild *Rosa chinensis* in its early flowering, small evergreen leaves and solitary pink flowers. A pretty rose, formerly sold in Paris as a pot rose and known since 1839. The climbing form reaches about 6ft (1.8m) tall and is best grown through another shrub. It is pretty with a Deutzia or Ceanothus which flower at the same time, or with the later-flowering *Solanum jasminoides*.

Rosa chinensis 'Viridiflora'

'Mutabilis'

'Comtesse du Cayla'

'Irene Watts'

'Mutabilis', 'Tipo Ideale'
One of the most
charming of all Old Roses
with masses of single
flowers which open pale
apricot before
becoming pink, in
loose, branched,
red-twigged
heads. They are
produced
throughout
the flowering
season until
Christmas or
the first serious frost; they
have only a slight fragrance. It
forms a robust bush to 7ft (2m) or
more if grown on a warm wall where
it will form strong woody shoots.
Of unknown origin, but probably
an old Chinese garden rose.
Although it was first recorded in
Italy in 1896, there is said to be a
painting of it by Redouté in Paris
which dates it from before 1836.

'Mutabilis'

'Le Vésuve', 'Lemesle'   Another lovely rose with
similarities to 'Mutabilis' and to the Tea roses,
raised by Laffay in France in 1825. It makes a stiff,
twiggy bush to 5ft (1.5m) tall, but often less, with
red twigs, the older stems clad in strong, sharp
thorns. The shapely red buds open into rich,
lightly-scented pink flowers, the outer petals
remaining red, the whole flower nodding

An exceptionally fine bush of 'Le Vésuve' at Mottisfont

'Rival de Paestum'

gracefully. I have found this an excellent rose which flowers continuously until the winter and is hardy and free from disease. Plant 3 or 5 together to form a really fine bush.

'Comtesse du Cayla'   A China hybrid raised by Guiot in France in 1902. The flowers are semi-double, well scented and produced regularly throughout the season. A small plant, usually less than 3½ft (1m) tall.

'Irene Watts'   A relatively modern hybrid raised by Guillot in 1896, with well-shaped, fully double, lightly scented flowers throughout the season. A low plant rarely reaching more than 2ft (60cm), so it is ideal for the front of a border or other choice position.

'Rival de Paestum'   This rose has all the delicacy of a Tea rose, although it is usually classed as a China, or a Tea-China hybrid. A low grower with purplish young growth and creamy white, lightly scented flowers, which nod when fully open. Raised in England by Paul in 1848.

'Paul Ricault'

PLANTING & PRUNING HELP The climbing varieties need extra feeding and watering to grow into good-sized plants. Like pure China roses, these hybrids tend to be rather tender, probably hardy to 0°F (–18°C), US zones 7–10.

'Hermosa' Like an improved version of 'Old Blush', this has pink, fully double flowers of good substance with a delicate scent. It flowers particularly well in autumn, even in wet seasons when other roses fail. Slight scent. Raised by Marcheseau in France in 1840. In the bush form the stems reach 5ft (1.5m) and there is also a climbing sport on record.

'Paul Ricault' This China hybrid has the appearance of a Gallica or a richly coloured Centifolia, with large double, quartered cerise flowers, a green button eye and petals which fade to pale pinkish purple at the edges. Fragrant. Stems to 7ft (2m), often bent down under the weight of flowers. Raised in France by Portemer in 1845. Free-flowering, but only in early summer.

China Rose Hybrids

Once established in Europe, the China roses were soon crossed with other groups in order to retain their perpetual flowering and improve their scent, size and the substance of their petals. Those shown on this page are some of these early hybrids which have held their place in gardens until the present, and definitely do not belong to other groups such as Bourbons and Teas.

'Fantin-Latour'

'Fantin-Latour' A lovely rose with large flowers on arching stems on a large spreading shrub around 7ft (2m) tall. Not a typical member of any group, though possibly a China or a Tea crossed with a Gallica or Centifolia. The scented flowers are at first cup-shaped with the outer petals later reflexing. Leaves large and glossy. Of unknown origin, but recorded in 1900.

'Sanguinea'

Climbing 'Cécile Brünner' in Fred Boutin's garden in Tuolumne, California

'Cécile Brünner'   A small-flowered rose with Tea rose leaves and perfect pale pink flowers in large heads throughout the summer. Raised in France by the Veuve Ducher in 1881. The branched heads of flowers are derived from the dwarf repeat-flowering *Rosa multiflora* and the elegant flower shape from the Tea rose 'Mme de Tartas'; the flowers are lightly scented. Height to 4ft (1.2m). There is also a strong climbing form which can scramble into a small tree. Other charming roses in this group include the pale yellow 'Perle d'Or' and the purplish pink 'Lady Ann Kidwell' raised in America in 1948.

'Sanguinea', 'Miss Lowe', 'Bengal Crimson', A single red China rose, becoming pink in cold weather. The good substance of the flowers, which can be around 3½in (9cm) across, and the leaves, suggest that this is a Chinensis-Gigantea hybrid. The same plant can either be a dwarf shrub to 2ft (60cm) tall or with support, grow up into a large shrub 10ft (3m) or more. The smaller-flowered forms are often called 'Miss Lowe'.

'Hermosa'

'Devoniensis'

'Parks' Yellow Tea-scented China'

Old Tea Roses

Among the roses introduced from China in the early 19th century was one with large delicate, pale pink flowers, which came to be known as 'Hume's Blush Tea-scented China'. This was the first of the dwarf repeat-flowering Tea roses in Europe. It was crossed with a second Chinese rose, a once-flowering pale yellow climber, 'Parks' Yellow Tea-scented China' and from them came an important group, the Teas, with flowers in delicate shades of pink, creamy yellow and apricot, of which some were dwarf, some climbing.

PLANTING & PRUNING HELP   Tea roses do best in the warm climates of California, the southern US and southern France and Italy. The climbing forms are better in colder climates, as they can be trained on a warm wall. They need very rich feeding and heat to reach their full potential. Pruning after flowering helps the production of later flowers. Hardy to 10°F (–12°C), US zones 8–10.

'Parks' Yellow Tea-scented China'   An old Chinese garden rose, sent from Canton to England by John Parks in 1824. Still a good rose, covering a wall with elegant leaves and in late spring, numerous pale yellow flowers with an occasional pinkish flush. Slight scent. Young leaves and stems red. Stems to 10ft (3m) or more.

'Devoniensis'   A Tea introduced in bush form in 1838 and as a climber in 1858. Foliage is close to 'Parks' Yellow', but stems green and flowers larger, whiter and flatter. It also flowers again in autumn. Stems eventually to 40ft (12m). Raised by G. Foster of Devonport near Plymouth, England, a cross between 'Smith's Yellow' and 'Parks' Yellow'.

'Sombreuil'   Generally classed as a Tea rose, although its parentage makes it a Hybrid Tea. Flowers flat and white, very double, scented, produced continually into autumn. Stems to 13ft (4m). Raised by Robert in France in 1850, from 'Gigantesque' × a Hybrid Perpetual.

'Marie van Houtte'   A Tea with large, nodding, pale yellow, fragrant flowers, raised by Ducher in France in 1871. Scent good and height to 6ft (1.8m) on a warm wall, lower in the open.

'Général Schablikine'   A Tea with quite small, slightly scented flowers of particularly rich colouring; the crimson buds opening to show pink petals with a deeper back. Open flowers rather loose, with a delicate scent. This excellent rose flowers almost continuously and will form a large shrub or climber in a mild winter climate, such as California, London or the Mediterranean. Raised by Nabonnand in France in 1878.

'Général Schablikine'

TEA ROSES

'Parks' Yellow Tea-scented China' at the Berkeley Botanical Gardens in April

'Sombreuil'

'Marie van Houtte'

'Général Schablikine' at Clos du Peyronnet, Menton

'**Bon Silène**' A lovely old Tea rose with rather small flowers similar to a China, raised by Hardy in France in 1835. Free-flowering and vigorous to 4ft (1.2m), with good scent. Rare in Europe, but available from Peter Beales and grown widely in California.

'**Francis Dubreuil**' A Tea with deep blackish red flowers and velvety petals, raised by Dubreuil in France in 1894. Good scent and grows to 3ft (90cm). Red is an unusual colour in the Teas with which this is usually grouped.

'**Senateur Lafolette**', 'La Folette' Raised by Busby, gardener to the 3rd Lord Brougham at Chateau Eléonore in Cannes in 1910. A mighty climber with sharp thorns, reaching 30ft (9m) or more with large, loose, fragrant flowers only in spring. Tender in England, but flowers well in a large unheated greenhouse. Its parentage was a Hybrid Tea crossed with *Rosa gigantea*, which was introduced by Sir Henry Collett from Burma and first flowered in Europe in 1898.

'**Mme Bravy**' A Tea rose with nodding, lightly scented flowers of the palest pink, produced in clusters. It is usually small, up to 3ft (90cm) and is famous as a parent of 'La France', which is said to be the first Hybrid Tea. Raised by Guillot of Pont Cherin in 1846.

'Mme Bravy' in the historic rose collection at Kew

'**Maman Cochet**' A lovely rose with red twigs and dark green, shiny leaves. The flowers are pale pink with a yellowish flush in the centre. There is also a beautiful white sport with creamy flowers, and reddish outer petals which is grown in California. Good scent and up to 4ft (1.2m) tall or more in the climbing form. Raised by Cochet in France in 1893.

'Bon Silène'

'Maman Cochet'

TEA ROSES

'Senateur Lafolette' at Clos du Peyronnet, Menton

'Senateur Lafolette' at Clos du Peyronnet

'Souvenir de Mme Léonie Viennot'
A climbing Tea with large, loose, apricot yellow
flowers, raised by Bernaix in 1898. Good scent and
flowering again in autumn. Stems to 20ft (6m)
tall; leaves large and glossy.

'Souvenir de Mme
Léonie Viennot'

'Francis Dubreuil' at La Mortola

'Mrs Oakley Fisher'

'La France'

'Ophelia'

'Lady Hillingdon'

Late Teas & Early Hybrid Teas

The Tea roses were delicate in other features as well as colour, needing a warm climate with rain in summer and little frost in winter. Rose breeders soon crossed them with other hardier groups, notably with the rather coarse Hybrid Perpetuals, to form the Hybrid Teas, the main group of modern large-flowered roses that has dominated rose breeding and production in the 20th century. The Hybrid Teas have proved adaptable to all but the harshest climates and are available in most colours. The few shown here are among the early ones and retain some of the delicacy of the old Teas.

PLANTING & PRUNING HELP
Feeding and warmth are the keys to success with these Old Roses. When pruning repeat-flowering roses after flowering, be sure to remove at least the top 2 or 3 leaves with the dead flower, and cut back feeble, non-flowering shoots even lower down. Most of these roses are hardy to 10°F (−12°C), US zones 8–10 or possibly a little lower.

'La France' A lovely rose raised in 1867 by Guillot fils and said to be a cross between the Tea 'Mme Bravy' and the red Hybrid Perpetual 'Mme Victor Verdier'. Later, in the 1880s, this was recognized as the first of the Hybrid Teas. The petals, which are paler inside, curl back from the high centre and the scent is heavier than that of most Teas. 'La France' makes a reasonable bush by

'Dove' in David Austin's rose garden in September

modern standards, up to 4ft (1.2m) or 10ft (3m) in the climbing form.

'Lady Hillingdon'   A fine rose, usually grown as a climber, with purple stems, young leaves and long flowers of rich creamy apricot with a delicate scent. These splendid flowers are produced throughout the season. Raised by Lowe and Shawyer of Uxbridge near Hillingdon in 1910, and the climbing form in 1917. A good plant may reach 20ft (6m), but 8ft (2.5m) is more usual. As hardy as a Hybrid Tea, although it is said to be a cross between the two Tea roses 'Madame Hoste' and 'Papa Gontier'.

'Ophelia'   Introduced by Wm. Paul and Sons of Waltham Cross in 1912, but of mysterious origin as it appeared in a batch of the Hybrid Tea 'Antoine Rivoire' sent from Pernet Ducher in France. 'Ophelia' is a lovely rose with perfect shape, white with undertones of pink and yellow. Well scented; to 3ft (90cm) or 15ft (4.5m) as a climber. It has also proved genetically very unstable in colour and a great producer of sports.

Two of these, 'Mme Butterfly' and 'Lady Sylvia', in shades of pale pink, are still popular in both bush and climbing form, and 'Golden Ophelia' is a good yellow.

'Dove'   Although modern in age, 'Dove' has much of the delicacy and charm of the Tea roses. Raised by David Austin in 1984 by crossing 'Wife of Bath' with a seedling of 'Iceberg'. A delicate arching bush around 3½ft (1m) across, with lovely greyish pink, lightly scented flowers throughout the season.

'Mrs Oakley Fisher'   Single roses have never had the popularity of doubles, although they must have had a brief spell of popularity from 1900 until the 1920s. This is still one of the loveliest of all roses, with large coppery yellow flowers throughout the summer. To about 3ft (90cm) tall and lightly scented. Raised by Cants of Colchester in 1921. Other lovely and still popular singles are the Irish group, led by 'Irish Elegance' raised by Dicksons of Ulster in 1905, and 'Dainty Bess' raised by Archer of Sellindge, Kent.

'Iceberg' with *Buddleia alternifolia* behind

'Paul's Lemon Pillar'

Classic Hybrid Teas

While most of the thousands raised have been lost, a few of the early Hybrid Teas have survived because of their distinct charm or tough constitution. Floribundas, now called Cluster-flowered roses have been similarly short-lived as breeders promote their new improved varieties.

'Comtesse Vandal'   A Hybrid Tea raised by Jackson & Perkins in 1932. Good scent. Stems to 3½ft (1m). Of classic parentage ('Ophelia' × 'Mrs Aaron Ward') × 'Souvenir de Claudius Pernet'. All three of these are still grown.

'Gruss an Aachen'   A lovely delicate rose with many of the characteristics of David Austin's modern English Roses. Of Hybrid Tea parentage 'Frau Karl Druschki' × 'Franz Deegen'. Repeat flowering with slightly nodding flowers on stems to 3½ft (1m). Raised by Philipp Gedulig of Kohlscheid bei Aachen in 1909.

'Iceberg'   Still one of the most planted white roses and excellent as a large shrub to 5ft (1½m) or 17ft (5m) in its climbing form. Flowers in clusters, cupped, with little scent, but produced reliably from summer to winter. Raised by Kordes in 1958 and the climbing form by Cant in 1968. Parentage: 'Robin Hood' (a Hybrid Musk) × 'Virgo'.

'Mrs Herbert Stevens'   A white Hybrid Tea raised by McGredy in 1910 and the climbing sport by Pernet-Ducher in 1922. Flowers produced throughout the season, well scented. Stems to 20ft (6m); bred from 'Frau Karl Druschki' × 'Niphetos' (a white Tea).

'Sutter's Gold'
A rich golden yellow or sometimes pinkish Hybrid Tea with well-scented flowers; the repeat-flowering bush form raised by Swim in 1950 to 3ft (90cm). Named after Sutter's Creek near Sacramento, where gold was first discovered in 1849. Parentage: 'Charlotte Armstrong' × 'Signora'.

'Sutter's Gold'

'Gruss an Aachen' at Hidcote

'Comtesse Vandal'   'Mrs Herbert Stevens'

'Paul's Lemon Pillar' A scented Hybrid Tea raised by Paul in 1915. Flowers white with a yellow flush and produced only in midsummer. A climber to 15ft (4.5m). Parentage: 'Frau Karl Druschki' × 'Maréchal Neil'.

'Virgo' A lovely white Hybrid Tea with long buds, raised by Mallerin and introduced by Meilland in 1947. A tough plant although susceptible to mildew, height to 2½ft (75cm) and some scent. Parentage: 'Pole Nord' × 'Neige Parfum'.

'Virgo'

'Claire Jacquier'

Noisettes

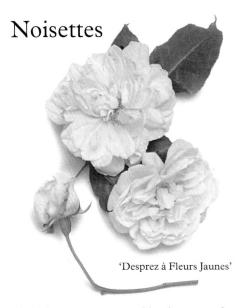

'Desprez à Fleurs Jaunes'

The Noisettes as a group combine the scent and late flowering of *Rosa moschata*, the cultivated Musk rose, with the large flowers of the Teas and Chinas. The original 'Blush Noisette' has masses of small double flowers. The later Noisettes,

crosses between 'Blush Noisette' and 'Parks' Yellow Tea-scented China' and other Tea roses, have larger flowers until they become almost indistinguishable from the Climbing Teas. Most will be hardy to 10°F (−12°C), US zones 8–10 or possibly a little lower.

PLANTING & PRUNING HELP   These roses are good in the greenhouse, producing flowers in April and May with little heat, and again in autumn. They do best planted in the ground, and associate well with reticulata camellias, coming out when the camellias are past. Climbers such as 'Maréchal Neil' may be trained along the roof and smaller varieties grown as standards or bushes. Detailed instructions on growing tender roses in greenhouses and in pots may be found in books published around 1900, when this type of cultivation was in vogue; try finding the *Country Life Century Book of Gardening*. Hardy to 10°F (−12°C), US zones 8–10 or a little lower.

'Aimée Vibert', 'Bouquet de la Mariée'   This rambling Noisette was raised by Vibert in France in 1828 and is thought to be a cross with the evergreen Mediterranean climber *Rosa sempervirens*. It is a useful plant for its late-season bouquets of flat, double flowers. Height usually to 15ft (4.5m). Some scent.

NOISETTES

'Blush Noisette' at Longleat House, Wiltshire

'Blush Noisette' This, the original Noisette rose, was a seedling of 'Champney's Pink Cluster', a cross between Old Blush China and the Musk rose, raised by Champneys in South Carolina in 1802. Seed of this was sent to France and produced 'Blush Noisette' in 1817. It is a good repeat-flowering rose, with clusters of small rounded flowers, palest pink from crimson buds, produced into winter, when the flowers are deeper pink. A good scent, likened to cloves. A tall shrub or climber with stems usually up to 7ft (2m), but sometimes to 17ft (5m).

'Aimée Vibert'

'Claire Jacquier' A very free-flowering climber producing bunches of pale orange-yellow flowers, fading to cream, mostly in midsummer but with a few later. Strong-growing to 33ft (10m). Raised in France by Bernaix in 1888. Some scent.

'Desprez à Fleurs Jaunes', 'Jaune Desprez' This was the first stage in the production of the larger-flowered Noisettes, 'Blush Noisette' crossed with 'Parks' Yellow', which was raised by Desprez in France in 1830. It is a repeat-flowerer with a good scent from its very double flowers of pale yellow or buff. Height usually to 15ft (4.5m).

'Aimée Vibert' with *Solanum crispum*

Large-flowered Noisettes

'Céline Forestier'

'Gloire de Dijon'

By this stage the Noisettes seem to have very little left of the Noisette ancestry, and have become almost pure Teas. They need a warm wall with careful treatment in cool climates, but are fine in warmer areas.

'Céline Forestier' A very full double pale yellow, with a good scent, raised by Trouillard in France in 1842. A tall climber for a warm area with stems to 15ft (4.5m). Flowers produced throughout summer and autumn.

'Gloire de Dijon'

'Gloire de Dijon', 'The Old Glory Rose' This is one of the all-time favourite climbing roses, growing well on a north wall, flowering throughout the summer and autumn, even in Scotland. Flowers pale creamy apricot, pinker in warm weather. Scent very good; stems to 15ft (4.5m). Raised in France by Jacotot, by crossing a yellow Tea rose with the Bourbon 'Souvenir de la Malmaison'. Good in Scotland and worth trying in US zone 8.

'Lamarque' In 'Lamarque' the same parentage as 'Desprez à Fleurs Jaunes' produced larger, paler flowers close to 'Devoniensis', but with fewer petals. Good repeat-flowering and with a very sweet scent. This is a good rose in warm climates such as California, where it can grow to 13ft (4m) or more; probably better in a greenhouse in England although I have not grown it myself. Raised by Maréchal in Angers, France in 1830.

'Maréchal Neil'

'Lamarque'

'Mme Alfred Carrière'

'Rêve d'Or'

'Maréchal Neil'   This is the epitome of the greenhouse rose, with solitary large, nodding flowers of soft yellow, a good scent and delicate pale green leaves. Raised in France by Pradel in 1864. I have found this easy to grow and free-flowering, although the plant needs very good soil and feeding to produce decent shoots. Perhaps this lack of vigour is actually an advantage, as the plant does not take over as do strong growers like 'Senateur Lafolette. Grows to 7ft (2m). The fragrant flowers appear mainly in spring, although with suitable care and feeding a second flush can occur in autumn.

'Mme Alfred Carrière'
Probably the most commonly grown Noisette. Free-flowering, the white flowers, with a flush of warmth in the centre, are well scented and produced in clusters from pink-flecked buds. Raised by J. Schwartz of Lyon in 1879. Growth vigorous to 20ft (6m).

'Rêve d'Or', 'Golden Dream', 'Golden Chain', 'Condesa da Foz'   One of the brightest of the Noisettes with bunches of quite large, scented yellow flowers, very double with the petals becoming quilled. Raised by Ducher in France in 1869. Flowers again in autumn. Stems to 12ft (3.5m).

'Rêve d'Or'

63

'Reine des Violettes'

Early Hybrid Perpetuals

Hybrid Perpetuals were the large-flowered garden roses of the latter half of the 19th century. They combine repeat flowering with large flowers, excellent scent and strong colours, with a preponderance of reds and purples which were rare colours in the Teas, also popular at the same time. Hybrid Perpetuals are hardier than Teas, but do seem to suffer badly from powdery mildew. The Hybrid Perpetuals or *Hybrides Remontants* as they are called in France, have a complex ancestry. 'Rose du Roi', a Portland × China hybrid appeared in 1816. It is repeat-flowering with large red flowers and excellent scent. In around 1835 'Rose du Roi' was crossed with hybrid Chinas (Gallica × China) and Bourbons (Autumn Damask × China), and the new class of Hybrid Perpetual was formed. 'La Reine' (*shown here*) was one of the earliest. Hybrid Perpetuals can be recognized by their huge, usually rather flat flowers and by the coarse leaves which grow almost up to the base of the flower. When well grown they can make large, striking shrubs. Later ones were bred for showing as single flowers, and

'La Reine'

'Général Jacqueminot'

'Empereur du Maroc'

the form and health of the shrub as a whole tended to be ignored.

PLANTING & PRUNING HELP Hybrid Perpetuals tend to throw long, strong shoots from the base, and these can be pegged down, to flower along their length the following year, or shortened by half to keep a more compact bush. Summer pruning should be light, as the autumn flowers come from the same shoots as those produced in spring. Rich feeding and ample water in summer produce healthy plants and better flowers. Hardier than Hybrid Teas, to 0°F (−18°C), US zones 7–10.

'Empereur du Maroc' Still one of the richest-coloured roses, opening deep red and velvety, becoming deep purple with age. Raised by Bertrand-Guinoisseau in 1858. Flowers very well scented, on stems to 4ft (1.2m). 'Louis XIV', sometimes classed as a China, is rather similar in colour but has flatter, smaller flowers on a smaller bush.

'Jules Margottin'

'Général Jacqueminot', 'La Brillante' A large red flower on a tall bush, raised by M. Roussel in Montpellier in 1853. Good scent and leaves generally healthy. Stems to 7ft (2m). This is a good, typical Hybrid Perpetual.

'Jules Margottin' Thorny, hardy and free-flowering, but otherwise unexceptional. This rose has, however, survived since it was raised by Margottin in 1853. Stems to 6ft (1.8m) tall and a good scent.

'La Reine' A rounded flower with incurved petals, raised by Laffay in 1842. Flowers mid-pink shaded with lilac, but with little scent. Stems to 5ft (1.5m) tall.

'Reine des Violettes' A strong grower, still loved for its changing flowers which open cerise before fading to violet, and are very sweetly scented. Raised by Millet-Malet in 1860. Stems, with few thorns, to 6ft (1.8m) tall.

'Eugène Furst'   'Mme Victor Verdier'   'Gloire de Ducher'

'Triomphe de l'Exposition'

and the autumn flowers, though lovely, are few. Stems to 8ft (2.5m), so they should be pegged down or trained on a wall or pillar. Raised by Ducher in 1865.

'Triomphe de l'Exposition'   Flowers pinkish red with a good scent. Stems to 5ft (1.5m) with red thorns. Raised by Margottin in France in 1855.

'Paul Neyron'   One of the largest flowered of all Old Roses, with huge, flat flowers of purplish pink and a good scent. Stems to 6ft (1.8m) with few thorns. Raised by Levet in 1869.

'Mme Victor Verdier'   Rounded flowers of a rich pinkish red are arranged in a loose head; they are well scented and produced through the summer on an almost thornless shrub to 5ft (1.5m). Raised by Verdier in 1863 and famous as one of the parents of 'La France' (*see page 56*).

'Souvenir du Docteur Jamain'   A rose famous for its very dark colouring and good scent, raised by Lacharme in 1865. Almost a climber, with stems to 10ft (3m). The flowers keep their colour better in a cool position.

'Eugène Furst', 'Général Korolkov'   A deep red with a large flat flowers with very good scent, raised by Soupert et Notting in 1875. Stems to 5ft (1.5m) tall.

'Gloire de Ducher'   A very large-flowered rose with rich purple flowers with a paler edge and an excellent scent. Unfortunately, the leaves are liable to mildew, as are many of the Hybrid Perpetuals,

'Mrs John Laing'   A pale pink with incurved petals, later curling back. Flowers large and well scented, in clusters of 3 or 4, and resistant to rain. Raised by Bennett in England in 1887. Plant short, to 4ft (1.2m) with small thorns.

'Mrs John Laing'

'Souvenir du Docteur Jamain'

'Paul Neyron'

LATER HYBRID PERPETUALS

'Champion of the World'

'Baron Girod de l'Ain'   One of those with wavy-edged petals, a sport of 'Eugene Furst', introduced in 1897. Flowers well scented in clusters, on stems to 5ft (1.5m).

'Champion of the World', 'Mrs de Graw' A good pink with a very double, quartered flower like an old Gallica, and good scent, flowering often better in autumn than in early summer. Stems arching, to 5ft (1.5m). Raised by Woodhouse in 1894 from 'Hermosa' × 'Magna Charta' which is a purplish Hybrid Perpetual.

'Frau Karl Druschki', 'Reine des Neiges', 'White American Beauty'   One of the few Hybrid Perpetuals which never fell out of favour. Large white flowers touched with pink outside, raised by Lambert in 1901. A strong upright bush to 7ft (2m). 'Merveille de Lyon' (a Hybrid Perpetual) × 'Mme Caroline Testout' (a Hybrid Tea).

'Hugh Dickson'   One of the best for general garden use, with long shoots to 10ft (3m), which respond well to pegging down. Raised by Dicksons in Newtownards in 1905.

'Hugh Dickson' at Mottisfont Abbey Garden, Hampshire

'Frau Karl Druschki'

'Roger Lambelin'

'Roger Lambelin' In this sport of 'Prince Camille de Rohan' the flowers have crinkled edges, outlined and streaked with white. Flowers, with a good scent, in loose clusters on stems to 5ft (1.5m); introduced by Schwartz in 1890.

'Hugh Dickson'

'Ferdinand Pichard' A striped rose, raised by Tanna in 1921, sometimes grouped with the striped Bourbons (*see pages 44–45*). A bushy shrub to 8ft (2.5m). Flowers well scented, in clusters in midsummer and autumn.

'Ferdinand Pichard'

'Baron Girod de l'Ain'

69

Old Climbers

The first Hybrid Tea roses were valued as repeat-flowering bush roses. Soon, however, some of them mutated and produced climbing forms, similar in growth habit to their climbing Tea rose ancestors. Others on this page were raised as Climbers from different parents, but retain the large flowers associated with Hybrid Teas.

PLANTING & PRUNING HELP
These Climbers need rich soil and ample water in summer to produce their best flowers. In dry climates the second flush of flowers often coincides with the autumn rains. Pruning can be minimal; simply cut back old flowering side shoots and any stems which are too weak to flower. They vary in hardiness according to their parentage.

'Guinée'

'Cupid' A lovely, single, pale pink Hybrid Tea raised by Cant in Colchester, Essex in 1915. Once-flowering with a good scent and with a good crop of hips in autumn. Stems to 17ft (5m) tall or more. Hardy to 0°F (−18°C), US zones 7–10, perhaps.

'Guinée' Still one of the darkest of the Hybrid Tea Climbers, raised by Mallerin in France in 1938. Scent very good, flowering mainly in summer with some flowers later. Stems to 17ft (5m). Hardy to 0°F (−18°C), US zones 7–10.

'Paul's Scarlet Climber'

'Cupid'

CLIMBING ROSES

'Mermaid'   A lovely single yellow rose raised by Paul in 1918. A Tea rose crossed with the Chinese climbing species *Rosa bracteata*, and therefore not very hardy, surviving in 10°F (−12°C), US zones 8–10 and best in warm climates such as the Mediterranean and California. A vigorous and healthy climber to 33ft (10m), with some scent. Flowers produced mainly in summer, with a few continuing through to autumn. Leaves shiny and almost evergreen.

'Mme Caroline Testout'   A reliable old Hybrid Tea, with clusters of large blousy sugar pink flowers, raised by Pernet-Ducher from 'Mme de Tartas' × 'Lady Mary Fitzwilliam' in 1890. The climbing sport, with stems to 20ft (6m), was introduced in 1901. Flowers, with only slight scent, appear mainly in summer, with a few later. Hardy to 0°F (−18°C), US zones 7–10.

'Mme Grégoire Staechelin', 'Spanish Beauty' A lovely rose with many of the characteristics of a *gigantea* hybrid, raised in Spain by Pedro Dot in 1927. Flowers large, loosely double, nodding, scented, produced in late spring only. Leaves evergreen, shiny and pale green. Stems to 20ft (6m) when well grown, but on poor soil often less, reaching only around 7ft (2m). Parentage: 'Frau Karl Druschki' × 'Chateau de Clos Vougeot'.

'Paul's Scarlet Climber'   One of the commonest red Climbers with stems to 20ft (6m), flowering throughout the summer and into early winter. Flowers of medium size in clusters, with little scent. This has Rambler parentage (*Rosa wichuraiana* × Hybrid Tea), but is usually grouped with the Hybrid Teas because of its relatively large flowers.

'Mme Caroline Testout'

'Mme Grégoire Staechelin'

'Mermaid'

'Mermaid'

'Adélaïde d'Orléans' at La Bonne Maison, near Lyons

Old Ramblers

What is the distinction between a Rambler and a Climber, two terms commonly used for tall-growing roses? Both climb up trees or can be trained on high walls. David Austin distinguishes Ramblers as those once-flowering roses which produce masses of small flowers, while Climbing roses have large flowers in smaller groups, and often flower in autumn as well as in midsummer. As in all aspects of nature, there are areas of overlap, and some of the roses included here under Ramblers have flowers almost as large as those included in the sections on Noisettes and Climbers. Most Ramblers originated as crosses between Wild roses of the Synstylae group, so-called because their clusters of single white flowers have styles joined together into a spike-like style in the centre of the flower. The Synstylae are all white-flowered Rambling roses, putting out long shoots every year, which then produce sprays of scented flowers from each leaf bud. When crossed with Teas and Hybrid Teas, the Synstylae roses produced the Ramblers; few roses make such a fine show, though most are only once-flowering.

The earliest of the Synstylae to be used for hybridization was the native English Musk rose *Rosa arvensis*, which has rather few flowers in a group; it produced the Ayreshire rose 'Splendens'. Later came the eastern Musk rose *Rosa moschata*, which produced the Noisettes (*see page 60*). Later breeders used the Mediterranean Musk rose *Rosa sempervirens*, which produced Ramblers such as 'Adélaïde d'Orleans'. Next the Chinese Musk rose *R. multiflora* was introduced to Europe and from that another group was raised, of which 'Crimson Rambler' and 'Goldfinch' are examples. Later still the Japanese roses *R. wichuraiana* and *R. luciae* were brought to Europe, and these led to another distinct group with very shiny leaves, which includes 'Albéric Barbier'.

PLANTING & PRUNING HELP   Ramblers vary in their hardiness according to the hardiness of their wild parent. Pruning, after flowering or in winter, should aim to cut out the wood which has flowered and tie the new shoots into position.

'Adélaïde d'Orléans'   A very pretty Rambler with semi-double creamy white flowers from a pinkish bud, scented of primroses and produced

'François Juranville'

in early summer only. Evergreen, susceptible to mildew and not very hardy, surviving usually to 10°F (–12°C), US zones 8–10. A *Rosa sempervirens* cross raised by Jacques, gardener to the Duc d'Orléans in 1826. Stems to 20ft (6m). Needs a warm position and good soil to do well, but should be good in areas with summer drought.

'Albéric Barbier' One of the most satisfactory Old Roses for a dry or hot position. I have seen it covering a gigantic arbour in Turkey, and thriving in an old village in the south of France. It usually reaches about 15ft (4.5m). It was raised by Barbier of Orleans in 1900, a cross between evergreen Japanese *Rosa luciae* and a Tea 'Shirley Hibberd'. Flowers pale yellow in bud, very double, on reddish stalks but only lightly scented; leaves shiny, the leaflets widely spaced. Min. –30°F (–35°C), US zones 8–10.

'Félicité Perpétue' Small, fully double flowers in large clusters and a fetching name make this a favourite rose. Some scent. A sister seedling of 'Adélaïde d'Orleans', raised by Jacques in 1827, and named after his daughters. Stems to 15ft (4.5m). Late-flowering and good on a north wall.

'Flora' Another Jacques Rambler, dating from 1830, with relatively large, fragrant, pink flowers in summer only. A hybrid of *R. sempervirens*, with stems to 13ft (4m).

'François Juranville' A good fully double flower of orangy pink with good scent makes this an unusual and valuable Rambler. Once-flowering with long thin stems to 20ft (6m). Raised by Barbier of Orleans in 1906, by crossing *R. luciae* and the Tea 'Mme Laurette Messimy', usually classed as a China and thus of parentage similar to 'Albéric Barbier'.

'Félicité Perpétue'

'Flora'

'Albéric Barbier'

'Alexandre Girault'

'Amadis'

China roses in a temple on Mount Omei, China

'Mme de Sancy de Parabère'

'Amadis', 'Crimson Boursault' The Boursault roses are supposed to have originated from crosses between early China roses and *Rosa pendulina*, a small species from the Alps. They are thornless, hardy and do well in cold areas, with some scent but otherwise unexciting. 'Amadis' has red China-like flowers on long arching thornless canes to 17ft (5m). Raised by Laffay in 1829.

'Albertine' A very popular scented rose both for its bright colouring and great freedom of flowering. Raised by Barbier of Orléans in 1921 by crossing *R. luciae* and the Hybrid Tea 'Mrs Arthur Robert Waddell'. The perfect buds are bright pinkish orange, opening to shades of pale pink with a yellowish centre. Stems to 20ft (6m), best trained along a fence or hedge, with glossy leaves. Not very hardy and is killed in the coldest winters in Kent and central England.

'Fellenberg', 'La Belle Marseillaise' Roses scramble through the hedges of several of the old temples on Mount Omei in SW China. Most resemble 'Fellenberg', with loose red flowers with white streaks. It was said to have been raised by Fellenberg in 1857. The long arching stems reach about 7ft (2m) tall.

'Fellenberg'

'Mme de Sancy de Parabère'
A pink semi-double, lightly scented Boursault with broad, dark green leaflets and large flowers, produced only in summer. A climber to 17ft (5m), without thorns, raised by Bonnet in 1874.

LARGE-FLOWERED RAMBLERS

'Blush Boursault'

'Russelliana', 'Old Spanish Rose', 'Souvenir de la Bataille de Marengo', 'Russell's Cottage Rose' A strong climber in good soil, and will grow and flower well even in the poorest soil, with stiff thorny canes and clusters of sweetly scented, Damask-type roses. The eye is often green, the centre purplish red, fading to pink and white on the edges. Stems to 20ft (6m). Known since 1840, though of uncertain origin, possibly a climbing Damask × *Rosa arvensis*.

'Blush Boursault', 'Calypso' A pink Boursault with thornless canes to 17ft (5m) and flowers with little scent. Known since 1848.

'Alexandre Girault' Another of the excellent Barbier Ramblers, raised in 1909 by crossing *R. luciae* and the Tea 'Papa Gontier'. Stems to 20ft (6m), flowers double, in bunches with a scent likened to apples; once-flowering.

'Albertine'

'Russelliana' in California; this was used as a stock and is often found in hedges and abandoned yards

'Rambling Rector' at St Albans

'Goldfinch'

Multiflora Ramblers

Rosa multiflora is another Chinese rose, a scrambler through hedges, with a rather tight cluster of small white or pink flowers. The first significant introduction of the species was a garden form, the 'Seven Sisters Rose', in which the flowers changed colour after opening to give a mixture of pinks on one cluster. This came from Japan in 1817, and a darker red, the 'Crimson Rambler' came in 1878. Several new roses were bred from these in the early 20th century.

'Violette'

PLANTING & PRUNING HELP   Most of these roses produce long leafy shoots during and after flowering. In winter, cut out the old flowering shoots and tie in as many of these long shoots as are needed. They will produce the next season's flowers. Hardy to $-10°F$ ($-23°C$), US zones 6–9.

'Blush Rambler'   Raised by B. R. Cant of Colchester, Essex in 1903 by crossing 'Crimson Rambler' with 'The Garland', an old white-flowered Rambler with *R. moschata* parentage. Flowers cupped and with a good scent. Leaves pale and even yellow-looking on chalky soils, but still very vigorous with almost thornless canes to 15ft (4.5m).

'Goldfinch'   A yellow Rambler, tolerant of shade and good for climbing up an old tree. Flowers in clusters with the yellow buds opening cream with a central mass of golden stamens. Scent good. Stems to 17ft (5m). Raised by Paul in 1907, from a complex cross involving 'Crimson Rambler' and a Hybrid Tea.

'Kew Rambler'   An attractive, single-flowered Rambler with bright pink flowers and a white centre. Good scent. Stems to 20ft (6m), with

'Sanders' White Rambler' in Eccleston Square

'Sanders' White Rambler'

'Kew Rambler'

greyish leaves. Raised at Kew in 1912 from *Rosa souliei* × 'Hiawatha' (a Rambler close to 'Dorothy Perkins').

'Rambling Rector'   A very strong-growing, white-flowered Rambler; flowers semi-double with a good scent, which is carried on the air. Stems very thorny, to 40ft (12m). Of unknown origin and first recorded in 1912. Possibly *R. moschata* × *R. multiflora*.

'Sanders' White Rambler'   A white-flowered Rambler with small flowers and shiny leaves, close to 'Dorothy Perkins'. Raised by Sanders in 1912. Rather late-flowering with a good scent and stems to 13ft (4m).

'Violette'   There have been many attempts to produce a blue rose and this is one of the most blue. The little double flowers are a purplish colour, especially as they fade, have little scent and often have one white-streaked petal. Stems almost thornless, to 13ft (4m). Raised by Turbat in 1921. Other purple Ramblers include 'Veilchenblau', with semi-double flowers, and 'Rose-Marie Viaud', with lovely double pompoms of magenta, fading to greyish pink.

'Blush Rambler'

'Dorothy Perkins'

American Ramblers

Most of the French Ramblers were not hardy in eastern North America, so American breeders raised their own hardier varieties. Some used the pink-flowered Prairie rose *Rosa setigera*, native of the Midwest from Ontario to Nebraska, south to Texas and Florida; others used a hardier form of *Rosa wichuraiana* from Japan, which had the advantage of small, shiny leaves. In each case, the crossing of a large-flowered rose with the small-flowered Synstylae gave the typical growth and flowers of the Rambler.

PLANTING & PRUNING HELP These roses are very easy to grow and good on their own roots; they are mostly late-flowering. Pruning is as for Ramblers described earlier, although in wild areas of the garden they can be left to grow into huge shrubs or cover trees.

'American Pillar' A bright pink, single-flowered rose, raised by Walter van Fleet at the U.S.D.A. in Glenn Dale, Maryland in 1902, by crossing a *R. wichuraiana-setigera* hybrid with a red Hybrid Perpetual. Stems to 17ft (5m). No scent, susceptible to mildew and late-flowering, but still one of the most popular Ramblers for its reliable show of flowers. Hardy to −20°F (−29°C), US zones 5–9.

'Baltimore Belle' A very pretty old hybrid raised by Samuel and John Feast in Baltimore in 1843, using *Rosa setigera,* but producing a result close to the *sempervirens* Ramblers. Flowers well scented, very pale, double, in large loose hanging bunches late in the season. Stems to 17ft (5m). Hardy to −20°F (−29°C), US zones 5–9, perhaps.

'May Queen'

'Baltimore Belle'

'May Queen' on the bothy at David Austin's nursery

'Dorothy Perkins' This is the most familiar of all Ramblers in cottage gardens in England and immediately recognizable by its small, well-scented, pink double flowers with mildew on the flower stalks, which become paler as they fade. As a pergola rose it can reach 12ft (3.5m) but much larger if allowed to sprawl along a hedge. It was raised in 1901 by Jackson and Perkins, who are still one of the largest rose breeders in America, by crossing *Rosa wichuraiana* with 'Mme Gabriel Luizet', a Hybrid Perpetual. It is perfect for covering a fence or pergola. Remove the old wood after flowering and carefully tie in the new canes. 'Excelsa', sometimes called 'Red Dorothy Perkins' is very similar, with bright pinkish red flowers.

'May Queen' Roger and I were most impressed when we saw this rose covering an old barn at David Austin's nursery. The double flowers are old-fashioned in shape, pale pink with a deeper centre, and have a good scent, but only come in summer; May is rather optimistic for England, mid-June is more realistic. Stems can reach 17ft (5m). Raised in 1898 by crossing *R. wichuraiana* with a Bourbon. Probably hardy to −10°F (−23°C), US zones 6–9.

'American Pillar' with flowering fennel

79

'Cornelia' in Brompton Cemetery, London

'Penelope'

'Felicia'

Hybrid Musks

Hybrid Musk roses are a small group which contains some of the very best of all roses for garden use. They make good shrubs and many of them flower well a second time after the wonderful midsummer show. They are well scented with masses of medium-sized flowers in white, cream, pink, buff and red. Hybrid Musks have always been associated with the Rev Joseph Pemberton of Havering-atte-Bower in Essex, who died in 1926. He was an early fancier of Old as opposed to contemporary roses and by crossing 'Trier' (*see page 81*) with various Hybrid Teas, Pemberton produced the Hybrid Musks. 'Trier' itself was a large shrub, very well scented and repeat-flowering, characteristics found in most of Joseph Pemberton's hybrids.

'Cornelia'

'Buff Beauty'

PLANTING & PRUNING HELP   If the roses have been planted from containers, dig them up in late winter, shake off all the old compost, cut back the roots, add plenty of fresh soil and replant. Rose roots respond to pruning in the same way that stems do. They grow away in spring with renewed vigour. These roses respond well to good feeding, even when established. Little pruning is needed apart from thinning the older wood to make room for the new to encourage long arching shoots if you want to encourage that habit. Less pruning gives earlier flowers in smaller heads; hard pruning gives later flowers in large heads and is used if the plants are to be moved, are weak or only newly planted. Hardy to −20°F (−29°C), US zones 5–9.

'Trier'

'Buff Beauty'   One of the best of all garden roses with clusters of hanging flowers, fully double and well scented. Flowers buff, fading to cream and produced throughout the season. A tall or spreading shrub to 7ft (2m) tall and wide. Introduced in 1939 by J. A. Bentall, who was Pemberton's gardener, and continued introducing roses after Pemberton's death.

'Trier'   This is the parent of Pemberton's Hybrid Musks. It is a delicate large shrub or climber, with loose heads of pale creamy flowers with an excellent, heavy scent. It was raised by Peter Lambert in Germany from a seedling of 'Aglaia'. 'Aglaia' itself was a hybrid between the Noisette 'Rêve d'Or' and *Rosa multiflora*, so 'Trier' has much in common with the early, small-flowered Noisettes. Stems to 8ft (2.5m).

'Cornelia'   Smaller flowered and pinker than 'Buff Beauty', with pretty flat flowers and a sweet, heavy scent. The flowers are pale pink in summer and richer coloured in the cooler days of autumn. A spreading shrub to about 8ft (2.5m). Raised by Pemberton in 1925.

'Felicia'   A strong-growing shrub to 7ft (2m) with bunches of medium-sized buff pink flowers. A prolific flowerer with scented flowers in summer and autumn. A hybrid of 'Trier' and Hybrid Tea 'Ophelia', raised by Pemberton in 1925.

'Penelope'   Joseph Pemberton introduced this creamy yellow Hybrid Musk in 1924, from the same parentage as 'Felicia'. It is a vigorous shrub with stems to 7ft (2m) and loose heads of well-scented, semi-double flowers from pinkish orange buds. The leaflets are distinctly broad.

'Francis E. Lester' at Stancombe Park, Gloucs.

'Ballerina' This pretty single rose bears a close resemblance to *Rosa multiflora*. The masses of small flowers are produced from summer to autumn, and are pale pink from deeper buds. It forms a low bush with shoots around 4ft (1.2m) tall. Raised by Pemberton and introduced by Bentall in 1937.

'Erfurt' A low shrub to 3½ft (1m) with loose, soft pink flowers produced throughout the season. Young leaves coppery red. Raised by Kordes in 1939 from 'Eva' × 'Perle des Jardins'.

'Francis E. Lester' A single-flowered climbing shrub with large loose heads of well-scented pale pink flowers, which become white as they fade. Stems to 17ft (5m). Hips small and red. Raised at Lester Rose Gardens, US, in 1946, from the single pink Hybrid Musk 'Kathleen', one of Pemberton's early introductions.

'Fritz Nobis' A German hybrid of the Eglantine rose, with many similarities to a Hybrid Musk, raised by Kordes in 1940. It has one superb flowering of soft pink double flowers with a good scent, on a tall shrub with shoots to 7ft (2m) or more. The parentage is the Hybrid Tea 'Joanna Hill' × 'Magnifica', a seedling of *Rosa rubiginosa*.

'Will Scarlet' This is a sport of Kordes' rose 'Wilhelm' and is a bright scarlet compared with the deep purplish red of its parent. It was introduced by Graham Thomas in 1950. The flowers are semi-double with a delicate scent and the stems to 7ft (2m).

'Moonlight' A semi-double, pale yellow Hybrid Musk raised by Pemberton in 1922. Stems to 7ft (2m) or more. Flowers rather small, but well scented and produced in loose heads, the autumn ones larger than those formed in spring. Parentage: 'Trier' × 'Sulphurea'.

'Fritz Nobis'

'Moonlight'

'Ballerina'

'Erfurt'

'Will Scarlet'

Rosa pimpinellifolia wild on limestone in southern France

Wild Roses & their Hybrids

Although there are about 150 species of wild rose, less than 10 have gone into the making of all the thousands of cultivated roses. The last section of this book covers a few of the species which have been ignored or little used by rose breeders; some are old garden roses, long grown in China, Persia or Europe; others are wild species introduced into gardens in the 20th century. Most have small single flowers and flower only once, in midsummer.

PLANTING & PRUNING HELP
The varieties of *Rosa foetida* and *Rosa xanthina* originate from dry areas of central Asia and are very susceptible to blackspot. In humid areas plant them in a windy spot where the air circulation is good. *R. pimpinellifolia* and its forms, however, are tolerant of cold and damp; good for northern gardens and sandy soils. These species need little pruning.

Rosa pimpinellifolia *Rosa spinosissima*, 'Scotch Rose'   The wild form of this rose is common on sand dunes and rare on dry hills inland in many parts of England and western Europe, from Iceland to Russia. It is easily recognized by its pale yellow flowers, small rounded leaflets and blackish shiny hips. It is very hardy, and will grow and flower on the poorest soils; as a result, the cultivated varieties often persist on roadsides and in abandoned gardens. These old garden varieties of the 'Scotch Rose' include pinks, whites and yellows, singles and doubles; some are probably mutants, some are hybrids with other wild roses. Hardy to −30°F (−35°C), US zones 4–8.

***Rosa pimpinellifolia* 'Double White'**   An old variety, known since the late 18th century.

***Rosa foetida* 'Bicolor'**, 'Austrian Copper'
Rosa foetida is a bright yellow rose found wild from Turkey east to Pakistan and in Central Asia. In 'Bicolor' the flowers are yellow outside, but bright orange inside. This is an old Turkish variety, recorded in the 12th century, and brought first to Vienna from Constantinople, hence its association with Austria. All varieties of *Rosa foetida* grow best in dry, warm areas such as inland California and the drier western US, Australia and southern Europe. Hardy to −20°F (−29°C), US zones 5–9.

***Rosa foetida* 'Persiana'**, 'Persian Yellow'
Another ancient Eastern garden rose, brought to England from Persia in 1837. This brought the

Rosa foetida 'Persiana'

Rosa pimpinellifolia 'Double White'

strong yellows into modern roses and at the same time, the numerous spines and susceptibility to blackspot often associated with the older yellow roses. 'Harison's Yellow' is a hybrid between 'Persiana' and *Rosa pimpinellifolia*, with loosely double yellow flowers, raised in New York in the early 19th century. It was taken westwards across America by the pioneers and planted wherever they set up homesteads. Hardy to −20°F (−29°C), US zones 5–9.

'Canary Bird'   This excellent variety is one of the earliest to flower and one of the best yellow roses for English gardens. It appears to be a very good clone of *Rosa xanthina*, a native of northwestern China. The flowers are bright yellow, the leaves with usually 9 rounded leaflets. Very hardy to −30°F (−35°C), US zones 4–8. 'Helen Knight' and 'Golden Chersonese' are similar, but with smaller, deeper yellow flowers, and are hybrids with *Rosa ecae*, a small-flowered species from Central Asia.

'Canary Bird'

Rosa foetida 'Bicolor'

Rosa laevigata in the Jardin Exotique du Val Rahmeh, Menton

'Anemone'

Rosa bracteata, 'Macartney Rose'
An evergreen climber with neat white single flowers and leathery evergreen leaves. A native to China, introduced by Lord Macartney's embassy to Beijing in 1793. This rose is unusual for its long flowering season throughout late summer, and this characteristic was used by Paul to create the famous hybrid 'Mermaid'. Not hardy; can survive 10°F (−12°C), US zones 8–10.

'Cooper's Burma Rose'   The origin of this lovely single white rose is something of a mystery. It was raised at Glasnevin Botanic Garden, Dublin from seed sent from Burma. It appears to be a hybrid between *Rosa gigantea* and *R. laevigata* and has large loose flowers and shiny green leaves. A strong thorny climber to 33ft (10m) or more; if you can, tie in the long shoots which will then flower along their length the next year. Not very hardy, being damaged by temperatures below 15°F (−10°C), US zones 8–10.

Rosa bracteata

'Cooper's Burma Rose'

'Ramona'

Rosa laevigata

'Anemone' and **'Ramona'**   Two hybrids of *Rosa laevigata*, crossed with a Tea rose. 'Anemone' was raised by Schmidt in Erfurt, Germany in 1895 and 'Ramona', a deeper pink sport, was found by Dietrich Turner in California in 1913. Both are good once-flowering climbers to 13ft (4m), needing a warm wall in cool areas. Hardy to 15°F (–10°C), US zones 8–10.

Rosa laevigata, 'Cherokee Rose'   This rampant and thorny white climber was first described from Georgia, to which it had been introduced from China in the early 19th century. The leaves are evergreen and the hips bristly hairy. The fine white flowers are up to 4in (10cm) across. Not very hardy, being damaged by temperatures below 15°F (–10°C), US zones 8–10.

'Cerise Bouquet' at La Bonne Maison, near Lyon

Rosa villosa 'Wolley-Dod'

Large Shrub Roses

These large Shrub roses are wild species or hybrids of them. They have a single flowering in early summer and often a good crop of beautiful hips in autumn.

PLANTING & PRUNING HELP   These wild species need little pruning. In early spring the three-year-old shoots that have had hips the previous autumn can be cut away to tidy the bush. The plants should be well fertilized to encourage strong new shoots.

'Cerise Bouquet'   A lovely rose with large cerise flowers on slender stalks from long arching shoots. Of unique parentage, being a hybrid between the Chinese species *Rosa multibracteata*, and 'Crimson Glory', a large Hybrid Tea. Raised by Tantau and introduced by Kordes in 1958. Stems to 10ft (3m) long on a large specimen. Hardy to 0°F (−18°C), US zones 7–10.

Rosa roxburghii f. ***normalis***, 'Chestnut Rose' This unusual Chinese rose is easily recognized by its hips which are covered with green spines and topped by large, leafy sepals. The flowers are large

Rosa roxburghii

Wild *Rosa roxburghii* f. *normalis* in SW Sichuan, China

Rosa moyesii

and in various shades of pink in the wild, or very double in an ancient cultivated Chinese form. This rose eventually makes a rugged small tree with attractive peeling bark. The leaves have 9–19 leaflets. In western China this rose is common on banks between rice fields, where it gets ample water in summer. In gardens it needs a warm position. Not very hardy, being damaged by persistent temperatures below 10°F (−12°C), US zones 8–10.

Rosa villosa 'Wolley-Dod' *Rosa villosa* is a wild European species conspicuous in hedges and rough places in western and northern England and Scotland. It has greyish, downy leaves and often bright pink flowers, darker than those of an ordinary Dog rose. 'Wolley-Dod' is an extra-large version of *R. villosa*, with semi-double flowers and bright hips, an ideal shrub for a transitional area between the main garden and the wild. Very hardy to −20°F (−29°C), US zones 5–9. Col. A. H. Wolley-Dod of Edge Hall, Cheshire was the author of *A Revision of British Roses* (1931).

Rosa moyesii This Chinese mountain rose has deep pink or red flowers with golden stamens, followed by large, beautiful hips. The stems arch

outwards to around 20ft (6m) in a well-grown specimen, but usually nearer 10ft (3m). The small leaflets are widely separated. The hips are shaped like an old-fashioned beer bottle with a persistant crown of sepals. Easily grown in good moist soil. Hardy to −20°F (−29°C), US zones 5–9.

Rosa moyesii 'Geranium'
This selected clone of *R. moyesii* is slightly smaller with stems to 8ft (2.5m) and bright red flowers followed by rather fat hips. It was raised from seed at Wisley in 1938. Hardy to −20°F (−29°C), US zones 5–9.

Rosa moyesii 'Geranium'

89

Rosa filipes
'Kiftsgate'

Wild Climbing Roses

Although roses are generally thought of as shrubs, a large number of the wild species are climbers. Most of these have large heads of small white flowers and an excellent scent.

PLANTING & PRUNING HELP   Put large-flowered climbers to grow up among these small-flowered species and the two different sizes of flowers will set each other off. Pruning should be as for the Ramblers; simply cut out the shoots which flowered the previous summer in spring, before the new shoots begin to grow. Most of these roses, however, will be left to grow as they please, so sharp and hooked are their thorns.

Rosa banksiae 'Lutea'   This lovely old garden rose is a Chinese cultivated variety of a small-flowered single white. Its lovely pale yellow flowers open at the same time as Wisteria, with which it makes a good combination. A large climber to 50ft (16m) or more. Flowers around 1¼in (3cm) across, scented faintly of violets; double yellow in 'Lutea', single yellow in 'Lutescens', double white in var *banksiae* and single white in var. *normalis*. Easily grown, but not very hardy and shy to flower in cool summer climates. Do not prune away the old shoots; they continue to flower. Damaged by temperatures below 15°F (−10°C), US zones 8–10 for any length of time.

Rosa brunonii 'Betty Sherriff'   A lovely climber with long thorny stems to 30ft (10m), capable of covering a large tree or a castle wall. Flowers delicate, pale pink on opening. Thought to have come from Bhutan and named after the wife of the plant hunter George Sherriff. Raised at Edrom Nurseries, Berwickshire in around 1950. Probably hardy to −10°F (−23°C), US zones 6–9.

Rosa brunonii 'La Mortola'   Another cultivar of *Rosa brunonii* with large, bluish grey leaves and loose heads of large, scented white flowers. It is rather tender but one of the finest of this whole group, with individual flowers 1¾in (4.5cm) across. The seven rather narrow leaflets are finely velvety beneath. Probably introduced from NW ·Sichuan. Damaged by temperatures below 15°F (−10°C), US zones 8–10 for any length of time.

Rosa filipes 'Kiftsgate'   A well-grown plant of 'Kiftsgate' is one of the largest and most spectacular of all roses. Its powerful shoots climb into trees and cover buildings, producing huge heads of small, scented flowers on delicate stalks. The original plant of 'Kiftsgate' at Kiftsgate Court, Gloucestershire has climbed up a large beech tree to 30ft (9m) or more. Flowers to 1in (2.5cm) across, in heads to 18in (45cm) across. Hardy to −20°F (−29°C), US zones 5–9. *Rosa filipes* is native to western China, in Gansu and NW Sichuan.

Rosa multiflora   This small-flowered rose is an important parent of most cultivated roses. It is easily recognized by its rather long, pointed heads of small flowers, and by the fimbriate stipules which are narrow wings at the base of the leaf stalks. Wild *R. multiflora* is an arching or low climbing shrub with white or pink flowers. Double forms were long cultivated by the Chinese, as was a dwarf which continued to flower throughout the growing season on short shoots, instead of forming long arching shoots. This form became the parent of the Floribunda roses, and probably of the Hybrid Teas also through 'Old Blush'. Hardy, easily grown and self-seeding in parts of America; native to China. Hardy to −20°F (−29°C), US zones 5–9.

Rosa filipes 'Kiftsgate'

Rosa brunonii 'La Mortola' on the house at Knightshayes Court, Devon

R. banksiae 'Lutea' at the Chelsea Physic Garden

Rosa multiflora near Dali, Yunnan, China

Rosa brunonii 'Betty Sherriff'

Rosa multiflora

Rosa sericea f. *pteracantha*

Rose Hips & Autumn Colour

Rosa nitida A good dwarf suckering rose for a wet place, native to North America. Flowers bright pink; leaves shiny, bright red in autumn. Hardy to −30°F (−35°C), US zones 4–8.

Rosa davidii* f. *elongata A Chinese shrub with clusters of pink flowers and large red hips. In f. *elongata* the hips are especially long. Hardy to −10°F (−23°C), US zones 6–9.

Rosa sericea* f. *pteracantha A much-branched shrub with ferny leaves, solitary white flowers and small red hips. Hardy to 0°F (−18°C), US zones 7–10.

Rosa glauca A wild rose, native to the S Alps, its stems arch outwards to 10ft (3m) or more, the grey leaves studded with pink flowers, followed by bunches of bright red hips. Tolerant of some shade. Hardy to −30°F (−35°C), US zones 4–8.

Rosa rugosa A tough rose, native to the coasts of China and Japan and naturalised in sandy places elsewhere. Flowers naturally large, deep pink, but double and purple in 'Roseraie de l'Haÿ' and large pale pink and single in 'Fru Dagmar Hastrup'. Large fat hips are freely produced by the single varieties. The hardiest of garden roses. Hardy to −40°F (−40°C), US zones 3–8.

Rosa sericea f. *pteracantha* showing thorns

Rosa nitida showing autumn colour

Rosa davidii f. *elongata* with large hips in bunches

Rosa roxburghii f. *normalis*
(*see page 88*)

Rosa glauca showing the bluish grey leaves

Rosa rugosa

Rosa moyesii 'Geranium' (*see page 89*)

Rosa moyesii 'Geranium'

Index

INDEX